THE
FEAR
VIRUS

THE
FEAR
VIRUS

VACCINATING YOURSELF AGAINST
LIFE'S GREATEST PHOBIAS

ED YOUNG

NEW YORK TIMES BEST-SELLING AUTHOR

Published by Creality Publishing in association with The Fedd Agency, Inc., a literary agency.

Unless otherwise noted, all scripture quotations are taken from the Holy Bible, New International Version®, NIV®. Copyright © 1973, 1978, 1984, 2011 by Biblica, Inc.™ Used by permission of Zondervan. All rights reserved worldwide. www.zondervan.com The "NIV" and "New International Version" are trademarks registered in the United States Patent and Trademark Office by Biblica, Inc.™

Scripture quotations marked (NKJV) are taken from the New King James Version®. Copyright © 1982 by Thomas Nelson. Used by permission. All rights reserved. Scripture quotations marked (NLT) are taken from the Holy Bible, New Living Translation, copyright ©1996, 2004, 2015 by Tyndale House Foundation. Used by permission of Tyndale House Publishers, Inc., Carol Stream, Illinois 60188. All rights reserved.

Scripture quotations marked (NASB) are taken from the New American Standard Bible® (NASB), Copyright © 1960, 1962, 1963, 1968, 1971, 1972, 1973, 1975, 1977, 1995 by The Lockman Foundation. Used by permission. www.Lockman.org

Scripture quotations marked (MSG) are taken from THE MESSAGE, copyright © 1993, 1994, 1995, 1996, 2000, 2001, 2002 by Eugene H. Peterson. Used by permission of NavPress. All rights reserved. Represented by Tyndale House Publishers, Inc.

Scripture quotations marked (TLB) are taken from The Living Bible copyright © 1971 by Tyndale House Foundation. Used by permission of Tyndale House Publishers Inc., Carol Stream, Illinois 60188. All rights reserved. The Living Bible, TLB, and the The Living Bible logo are registered trademarks of Tyndale House Publishers.

Scripture quotations marked (BSB) are taken from The Holy Bible, Berean Study Bible. Copyright ©2016, 2018 by Bible Hub Used by Permission. All Rights Reserved Worldwide.

Scripture quotations marked (NHEB) are taken from the New Heart English Bible.

ISBN: 978-1-949784-43-5
eISBN: 978-1-949784-44-2

Printed in the United States of America

First Edition 15 14 13 12 11 / 10 9 8 7 6 5 4 3 2

TABLE OF CONTENTS

INTRODUCTION

I was standing in our kitchen next to my wife, Lisa, when the phone rang. It was my cardiologist. I looked at Lisa and remarked, "This can't be good." Over the next few moments, my doctor told me that one of the valves in my heart was not functioning properly. He explained that my heart had severe regurgitation, which means a backwash of blood was flowing the wrong way into my heart. The blood was also seeping into my lungs and into other areas. What was weird is that I was pretty much asymptomatic. I felt and looked healthy. It's surreal to hear that your life is in danger when you feel perfectly fine.

It wasn't a complete shock to me that my heart could one day be problematic. I was born with a heart murmur, so I regularly monitored my heart health since I was young. But I had never been critical or at risk for surgery. I was certainly not expecting the life-altering news that I was now a heart patient.

I still remember when someone first looked at me and said, "You're a heart patient."

I thought, "You've got to be talking to the wrong person. A heart patient? I've eaten clean, I was a college athlete, I've run a marathon, I work out with a trainer, and you're calling me a heart patient?" But as my condition became more critical and I was looking at surgery, I thought, "Yeah, that's true. I am a heart patient."

I would soon find out that mitral valve prolapse heart surgery is more complex than a typical heart surgery. So, I called my friend Manny, a cardiologist in Houston, and asked him for a second opinion. He looked at my tests and he said, "Ed, you need heart surgery fast. Your heart could have irreversible damage, and if you don't get it taken care of, you could die." Then he said, "There are only two people in the world I would recommend touching my heart, specifically the mitral valve. One guy is in Europe and the other guy works in my group. He's the renowned surgeon, Dr. Gerald Lawrie from Australia." I googled him and, sure enough, he is one of the top heart surgeons in the world. Sometimes we throw that phrase out flippantly: "best in the world." *That restaurant is the "best in the world." That university is the "best in the world."* But this guy, literally, was one of the best surgeons in the world for this type of surgery.

Manny arranged for me to see Dr. Lawrie. Lisa and I met with this master surgeon, and he explained the mitral valve prolapse surgery. He described what would happen: they would open me up, put me on a bypass machine, and then stop my heart. Yes, that is as scary as it sounds. Time stopped for a moment as I imagined myself going through the process. I felt like I was beginning a journey into the unknown. But I was not alone, of course. Lisa was with me, as well as our kids, family and friends, and our church. But in order to fix my heart, I would need to put my life in the hands of this expert. I made the decision to submit myself to this incredible heart surgeon and trust him with my life.

Was I afraid? Did I have some fear? Absolutely! And if I wasn't careful, fear would slowly suffocate me like the blood that was flowing into my lungs. Without intentional steps in such a literal life-and-death situation, I would soon drown in my own fear.

The truth is, all of us are heart patients. I'm not talking about the vital organ in your chest but the heart that is the seat of yourself, your intellect, your morals, and your spirituality. And because of sin, we are heart patients, vulnerable to sicknesses like fear. You may not know it, you may not feel it, but at this very moment you could have a severe case of the fear virus attacking your heart. You could be in danger right now of missing out on God's best for your life because fear is choking out your future. We all need to come to terms with the fact that we are heart patients and we have a fear virus that is taking life out of us. But there is a peace and joy God has for you—regardless of the circumstances in the world. Throughout this book, we are going address what is infecting us and talk about how to vaccinate our hearts and our lives against life's greatest fears.

Fear is often rooted in the inescapable fact that we are not as in control of our world as we think. Rarely does the entire world come to this conclusion at the same time. Yet in the first months of the new decade, our world was introduced to the COVID-19 virus. For generations to come, we will point to this virus as a reminder of how quickly we can lose control of our daily routines and lose confidence in what brings us security.

When the fear virus takes hold of our hearts, it starts seeping into every area of our lives, our relationships, our society, our dreams and thoughts. Fear comes at us in unexpected ways and is always jolting, like when I got the call about my heart, or when COVID-19 swept through continents and crossed oceans, causing universal fear.

Amidst the pandemic, everyone, to some degree, ceased living the life they knew and had to face the real fear of uncertainty. The media was on loop with information—some truth and some speculation—spiking fear into the population. Uncertainty breeds fear, and fear is a contagious virus. This pandemic revealed a deeper problem, a deeper issue: most of us have a natural bent toward fear, and we let that fear seep into our thoughts and every area of our lives until it controls us.

The perpetuation of fear comes through various carriers. Our contact with social media, the news, and opinion boards have our fears on full display, and we are playing them on repeat. One of the things we learned during the pandemic is that we needed a trustworthy source of information. News broadcasts and social media posts were not all reliable. Emotions would rise and fall over information that may or may not be true. The fear virus contaminates and spreads to every area of our life if we are not careful. In order to fight the fear virus in our lives, we need context and we need truth. Whether it is our finances, job security, health, or the future, we must have the truth so that we give proper context to our fears.

The Bible says in 1 John 4:18, "There is no fear in love. But perfect love drives out fear because fear has to do with punishment, and the one who fears is not made perfect in love." It comforts me to know that perfect love drives out fear and that God gives us the context and the truth we need in any circumstance where fear is present. When we look at our circumstances through the lens of God's perfect love, we will see with a new perspective made clear by the peace of God which will guard our hearts and our minds (Philippians 4:7). If I don't process my fear through the context of God's love, that fear will become the lens through which I see everything. The vision for my life will be distorted, absent of God's light and clarity. When we see the world through fear, that is when things get funky and freaky. That is when we start fighting people in grocery stores over toilet paper or the last box of Eggo waffles. But perfect love—love of God, a relationship with God—casts out fear. When we lean into the love of God and view the world through the lens of His love, we can realign our perspective to truth, even in the midst of a virus or a market crash.

The fear virus is very contagious, and we must be vigilant in order to avoid it and not give it to others. This virus infects us and makes us forget God's sovereignty, protection, and goodness. Those of us who believe in God know that He holds the future in His hands. What does that really mean, and how can knowing God help you in the face of fear? Whether you believe in God or not, I would hope we can all agree we are clearly not in control of our world. One germ wreaking havoc in every nation on earth should teach us that.

However, the Bible says that God is in control, that He is sovereign—and that should give us peace. Thinking we are sovereign leads to unnecessary stress and anxiety, growing fear, unhealthy coping, poor choices . . . the list goes on and on. The simple truth is God alone is in control and we are not.

When we let fear run the show, everything is based on insecure feelings and emotions. And it's not pretty. Fear can totally freak us out, dominate us, and lead us to make decisions based on false facts that are not rooted in reality. So often, the fearful thoughts and feelings we have are not based on real evidence. We are consumed with projections and drawn in by misinformation or worst-case scenarios. Therefore, a great definition of unhealthy FEAR is "False Evidence Appearing Real."

In the midst of fear and pain, we need to get historical, not hysterical. Whenever you're riddled with fear, whatever the fear is—the fear of heart surgery, the fear of living alone, the fear of rejection, the fear of snakes—look back to the promises of God and borrow blessings He has spoken over His people. When our present circumstances feel hysterical, go historical, and cling to those ancient promises. "God is for us, who can be against us?" (Romans 8:31). "God works out all things for the good of those who love Him" (Romans 8:28). As King David wrote in Psalm 23, we too can say "even though we walk through the valley of the shadow of death, we fear no evil because God is with us." And holding on to this truth will give you the strength to face the future; it will give you the antidote to the fear virus. Remember that God is on the throne. God is sovereign. He is Lord. He is in charge. He's bigger. He's broader. He's stronger than any germ or any painful situation. Any death. Any tragedy.

While we are told in the Bible not to fear the world around us, we are told to fear God. How is that any different than our notion of "False Evidence Appearing Real"? How is fear of God different than my fear of rejection or my fear of the coronavirus? You see, there is a difference between positive fear and negative fear. We have to have a healthy fear of God, but the word for "fear of God" in the Bible has a different meaning. This fear means reverence and ultimate respect for God. It's putting God in His proper place so perfect love, the love of God, can cast out all earthly fear. The Bible says in the book of Proverbs, "The fear of the Lord is the beginning of wisdom" (Proverbs 9:10). If you want wisdom, if you want discernment, if you want a good read even on the coronavirus outbreak, then redirect your earthly fears to the healthy and heavenly fear that honors God. Focus on the perfect love that casts out fear.

If we continue to live by fear, we will place ourselves in the position of God, which leads to devastating results. If, though, we love God first, if we fear Him and revere Him and realize that He's God and we're not, that's when life makes sense. When God becomes number one in our lives, then we begin to understand God's love. We will be able to see the path that He has for us. We'll have His wisdom, His comfort, and His peace, even when pain hits us out of nowhere.

What are the fears in your life that you are facing? The fears that you need to stop running from and meet head on with God's perfect love? As you name those other fears in your life, start by praying, "I know that the fear of God, which is healthy fear, is the beginning of wisdom. God, I want to fear you, to revere you, to put you in your rightful place. When I do that, then I know I can face this fear."

If negative fear is "False Evidence Appearing Real," what's positive fear? A healthy fear of God means "Facing Everything with Assurance and Reverence." As we fight this fear virus, we can face every day and everything that comes across our path with reverence for God and assurance that He holds all things together. We are heart patients, and He is the healer. We have the fear virus, BUT the fear of Him is the vaccine; through His perfect love, we will have victory over our fear!

CHAPTER 1

LITTLE MAN

FEAR OF HELPLESSNESS

When I was a little kid, I was fearful of this imaginary person I made up. I used to call him "the little man." I would come to my parents crying and repeatedly saying, "I saw the little man!" My mom would try to quell my fears by saying, "There's no such thing as the little man. He is not in your room, under your bed, in the closet, or standing in the hall." Regardless, I was thinking about the little man all the time.

The little man, the little man, the little man. I saw him everywhere.

Sometimes I would get in bed with my brother because I was afraid of the little man. I was completely helpless against him. One night, my mom had enough. Quite exasperated, she turned on all the lights and we explored the confines of my room and the full expanse of our house. "There's no little man here in the closet, there's no little man here under your bed, there's no little man in the attic. There's no little man!" My mind was blown. She was right!

In the end, my mom and I determined that the "little man"

was probably the vacuum cleaner I could see more clearly when the lights were turned on. When light breaks through darkness we can see more clearly that we have nothing to fear. That reminds me of Psalm 27:1: "The Lord is my light and my salvation—whom shall I fear?" When you know The Man, you don't have to fear the little man.

When the fear virus takes root in our hearts, it distorts our perceptions and leaves us feeling out of control. We fear the feelings of helplessness caused by fear, so we try to run away. We can't run away from our heart condition, the deep-rooted fear in our hearts, and pretend we are healthy; we have to do the painful work of submitting ourselves to God so that He can heal us.

No one has control in this life; we like to pretend we do but we don't. God holds our lives in His hands. When we feel helpless and feel like we have no control, when we feel that the little man is near, we can remember that we have nothing to fear because God is in control and we are not helpless because He is on our side and is fighting for us. When the fear of helplessness grips you and renders you terrified, you have to shine light on the darkness. You have to bring God in and allow Him to show you that you have nothing to fear. As I have penned these words and as you read them, it is my prayer that God will shine a bright light on all of our fears and reveal to us that we don't have to just live with the fear virus. Together we will discover that there is a vaccine, His name is Jesus. Let's learn how we can choose to inoculate ourselves daily with His truth, hope and love.

A FEAR FOR EVERYTHING

Everywhere we turn, we seem to find another thing to add to our growing list of phobias, fears, and anxieties. We even have extensive lists categorizing all of these modern-day phobias. There are more fears out there than you have probably ever thought possible—some of them odder than others. Allow me to list just a few examples of the bizarre things that we humans fear:

- Arachnophobia is the fear of spiders.
- Aerophobia is the fear of flying.
- Claustrophobia is the fear of confined spaces.
- Dentophobia is the fear of dentists.
- Glossophobia is the fear of speaking in public.
- Hamartophobia is the fear of sinning.
- Liaphobia is the fear of lying. Just kidding; I made that one up.
- Pentheraphobia is the fear of your mother-in-law.
- Ecclesiophobia is the fear of church.
- Pteronophobia is the fear of being tickled by feathers.
- Venustraphobia is the fear of beautiful women.
- Xanthophobia is the fear of the color yellow.
- Anuptaphobia is the fear of staying single.
- Blennophobia is the fear of slime. (I've got to say, I am not very keen on slime.)
- Gamophobia is the fear of marriage.

You won't believe this one:

- Luposlipaphobia is the fear of being pursued by timber wolves around a kitchen table while wearing socks on a freshly waxed floor. (I did not make that up.)

Fear is a fascinating subject, and not just because some fears are humorous. Fear is fascinating because it has two sides. There is a negative side to fear in that it can paralyze us and tyrannize our lives. It can keep us from being all that God wants us to be. But fear also has a positive side. Fear is able to stimulate and motivate us to greatness. It can drive us to do the things we know God wants us to do with the life He has given us.

I once owned a Jeep Cherokee Chief that I loved! It had some charm and lots of quirks. It smelled like a bait bucket because I used it to shark fish, and my battery would always die so I carried jumper cables around with me. One day, I was in front of our house and the Cherokee Chief wouldn't start. So, using my battery cables, I tried to jump my car off of my dad's car—a brand new, midnight blue Lincoln Continental. I hooked up the battery cables and started Dad's car. Then, I started the old Cherokee Chief and I began to floor it. To my shock and horror, I watched through sparks and smoke as the battery cables melted into the Cherokee Chief and then melted into my father's brand-new car. I had made a costly mistake and it wasn't pretty.

What happened? I got the positive on the negative and the

negative on the positive. That's what happens in fear. We can get positive fear on negative fear and negative fear on positive fear. We get our wires crossed.

Not all fear is bad. We have to have fear—a healthy fear of God. But the word "fear" in the Bible is a reverence of God. It's being in awe of God and putting God in His proper place. The Bible says in Proverbs 9:10, "The fear of God is the beginning of wisdom." So, if you want wisdom and discernment—even when you are petrified with fear—you need to focus your fear on God. So often, we fear everything but God instead of fearing nothing but God. When our focus is on God, He will fill us with His perfect love and there will be no room for unhealthy fear.

But what happens if I get my wires crossed? What if I begin to live by fear of circumstances instead of the fear of God alone? The word for the negative kind of "fear" in the New Testament is the Greek word *phobos*. It is where we get the word "phobias." If I just constantly fall into my phobias, that's when everything gets messed up. I get the positive on the negative and the negative on the positive, and the fear will cause our lives to melt.

Fear is real and raw, but it's often times "False Evidence Appearing Real." But the positive fear? That is "Facing Everything with Assurance and Reverence."

When I think about positive fear, it is simply awesome respect or reverence before God. We confess that God is God; He is sovereign, perfect, and holy. When I have that type of fear, it's a positive fear that will drive away the negative fear. If we love God first, if we fear Him and revere Him and realize that He's God and we are not, that's when life begins to make sense. We'll have wisdom and understanding. We'll be able to see the way God wants us to do life even when pandemics strikes and pain hits us out of nowhere. When we fear God, He will help us face all other fears.

Negative fear can often control us, but we never want to admit that because we like to be in control. That's why people hoarded toilet paper, hand sanitizer, and all the non-perishable food they could find in the wake of the coronavirus pandemic. When we give ourselves over to fear and start losing control, we grasp for any and all control we can get. However, in grasping for control, we start taking God off of the throne and we try to take His seat. In giving ourselves over to fear (False Evidence Appearing Real), we are saying, "God, we don't trust you in this situation. We don't trust your sovereignty. We have to make it on our own." Seems kinda silly to knock God off the throne over a couple of germs, huh? We have to fight against our natural proclivity toward fear. And the first way we do that is by naming our fears.

We, as humans, fear the unknown and the helplessness that the unknown brings. We don't want to appear weak or incapable. We want to be autonomous, self-sufficient, and independent. And this goes back to Adam and Eve in the garden. They wanted to be like God; they wanted to be powerful and self-sufficient. To a certain degree, self-sufficiency and independence are good things to seek. But when those things interfere with our willingness to recognize our dependency on God, our pursuit of independence can wreak havoc in our lives. We become prone to the fear virus because sooner or later, we know we can't control everything around us. When the fear of helplessness creeps in, we must name our fears, take our thoughts captive, readjust our posture, and actively put our trust in God.

NAME YOUR FEARS

Unnamed fears create anxiety, restlessness, and feelings of helplessness in us. We might find ourselves doing certain things without knowing why we are doing them. Our bodies and minds naturally seek coping mechanisms, even if we aren't aware of the reason we need to cope. For example, you might be unaware of your social anxiety, but every time you meet with someone you are always picking at something—tearing up a piece of paper, picking at your cuticles, playing with your keys. Those habits are your body's ways of coping with stress and fear. You might be unaware of your fear of abandonment, and every time you start a new relationship, you become really clingy and always need to be around the other person. Maybe you have an unnamed fear of clowns, and you haven't been to a carnival in years. Whatever it may be, the only way to face your fears and begin processing them is to recognize them and name them.

How do we name fears we aren't aware of? Great question. One way is to spend some time introspecting. Reflect on your recent behaviors at work, at home, in your relationships with family and friends, in your finances. Reflect on the media you've been consuming. Is it projecting the values you are trying to live out? Or is it causing you to be more fearful? Reflect on your view of God. Do you see Him as a loving Father, a taskmaster, a silent observer, or a teacher? What is your current view of Him? In your time of honest introspection, you can uncover a lot about what your fears are and how they're controlling you.

Another way we can begin naming our fears is by talking to the people who know us the best. Whether that is a parent, a friend, a mentor, or a child, ask them questions. Here are a few to start with:

- Do you see any evidence of fear in my life right now?
- In what areas of my life do you think I need to grow?
- Have the ways I've been treating you and responding to things been encouraging or discouraging to you?

Not going to lie, these are hard conversations to have. You need to approach these conversations with humility. Try not to get defensive. Listen. Reflect. And take your questions to God as well. We can pray, "God, is there any area of my life that I've been acting in fear? Please reveal my fears to me so that I can name them and bring them before your throne." God loves to help us grow, so when you pray this, expect a quick answer.

When we know and can name our fears, we can finally stop running from them. We can face them head on. Constantly running from fear can leave us exhausted and feeling quite helpless. We don't need to keep running. Stop. Listen. What is it you're running from? Name it and claim power over it in the name of Jesus because "in all these things we are more than conquerors through Him who loved us" (Romans 8:37). We don't have to be consumed by our fear because God is bigger than any and all fear. And He is on your side.

TAKE YOUR THOUGHTS CAPTIVE

When we name our fears, we are more quickly able to see how much of our thoughts revolve around those fears. We begin to catch the spirals of fear toward the beginning rather than being defeated by them after they've run their course. When we recognize fear in our thoughts, we must stop it in its tracks. We can't keep letting those thoughts have a permanent residence in our mind when they've never paid rent. We have to evict them. As Paul says, we have to "take captive every thought."

2 Corinthians 10:5 says, "We demolish arguments and every pretension that sets itself up against the knowledge of God, and we take captive every thought to make it obedient to Christ." When we begin contracting the fear virus, it starts infecting all of our thoughts; we have to take each thought captive and submit our fears to Christ. We must hand our fear over to God and replace it with a promise or attribute of God. We must remove and replace the fear with something better, otherwise we will be just as defeated as when we let the fear run amuck.

We have to be vigilant against "what ifs." When "what ifs" flood your mind and leave you feeling helpless, replace them with "God is" statements. What if I get sick? What if I lose my job? What if I can't provide for my family? Stop those thoughts in their tracks, give the fear to God, and replace those thoughts with: God is my healer. God is my good Father. God is my provider and protector. God is in control and I can trust Him. God is always with me.

Now, you may be thinking, "Take every thought captive! That's a full-time job!" No argument here. Our thoughts are as swift as a raging river. One minute I'm thinking about pizza, and then the next I'm thinking about that one mean thing I said to a friend when I was fourteen. The goal isn't to beat yourself up for missing one. No, the goal is to change your perspective. Once you start recognizing fearful thoughts here and there and replacing them with thoughts that are lovely, admirable, and beautiful, you will more naturally think of the things of God. It won't be such a battle to control your unruly thoughts. It's like training for a race. When you begin, you're out of shape, but the more you train and the more self-discipline you exercise, you're soon running thirteen miles—no sweat. But you must keep training and being self-disciplined, otherwise you'll quickly find yourself out of shape and starting the process all over again.

So how do you train to take those fearful thoughts captive? Read God's Word. It's chock-full of lovely and good things to meditate on. Watch what you consume. What your eyes see, your thoughts fixate on. Pray to God throughout the day;

bring Him into your inner monologues. Find what works for you. Maybe what works for you is setting reminders on your phone every few hours that prompt you to put your thoughts on God. Maybe it's writing verses down and placing them around your house and in your car. Find what works for you and stick with it.

READJUST YOUR POSTURE

When life's events and tragedies leave us fear-struck and helpless, we need to analyze and readjust our posture to reflect our rightful place in our relationship with God. Life has a way of knocking us down. We get thrown a curveball and we falter. Whether it's a virus or a tragic loss, these events have a way of striking us with fear and knocking us down to one knee. In this position, there are a few different reactions.

Some of us can be prideful. Because we fear others will view us as helpless, we try to stand back up as soon as possible, trying to prove to ourselves and others that we are okay.

Or, when knocked down to one knee, we fall flat on our faces into self-pity and a victim mindset. We let fear overtake us and we convince ourselves we are alone even though God is always with us. We don't understand why God would allow these things to happen; life feels out of control. Rather than submitting ourselves to God's control, we become obsessed with our helplessness. What did we do to deserve this?

Still others of us in this position completely freeze. We

become stuck in these events and try to figure out what we could have done differently and how we could have avoided this event or tragedy. We let fear paralyze us; we become afraid of moving at all because we don't want to make matters worse. We are stuck on one knee, unable to grow and flourish because we are trapped in the fear of helplessness that the past holds.

These are some natural postures we take after fear creeps into our lives. You've probably experienced all of them at one time or another. So, what posture should we have in response to the fear of helplessness that we all experience? When life's events knock us down to one knee, what should our response be? I think God would say, "Put the other knee down, and give me your life and your worship." Put the other knee down and say, "God, have your way in my life." We need to say, "God, I have not been putting you first in my life. I surrender my fear to you and ask you to change my life. God, I want to do a 180-degree turn, and only the power of Christ can make it happen."

The Bible says that one day we will stand before God, and everything in our lives that has not been built on Jesus Christ and His church will crumble. In the midst of fear and helplessness, we can try to hoard material resources and wealth, we can try to figure out everything out on our own, and we can try to save and soothe our egos. But in the end, all of that will crumble in the presence of God. However, if we spend our life on our knees, praying and seeking God in the midst of our helplessness, when we stand before Him one day, we will treasure that time with Him forever.

We know from God's Word that He uses catalyzing events like this to bring people to Him, to remind them of important realities in life. Jesus talked about one of these realities in Matthew 7:24-27:

> *Therefore everyone who hears these words of mine and puts them into practice is like a wise man who built his house on the rock. The rain came down, the streams rose, and the winds blew and beat against the house; yet it did not fall, because it had its foundation on the rock. But everyone who hears these words of mine and does not put them into practice is like a foolish man who built his house on sand. The rain came down, the streams rose, and the winds blew and beat against the house, and it fell with a great crash.*

Christ was talking about an eternal foundation here. He was contrasting those who are authentic disciples of His with those who are not. Those who do obey His teaching and surrender control to Him are like the wise man who builds on the rock, and those who do not obey Him and try to do life on their own are like the foolish man who builds on sand.

Many people today are building their lives on treacherous foundations. Their lives are characterized by striving for control while being controlled by inner fears—because they are one storm away from disaster. They have trappings of religion, but there is no genuine fruit to indicate any evidence of an authentic relationship with Jesus Christ. Instead, their lives are built on power, wealth, status, family, or country. Jesus' parable of the wise and foolish man leads us to the question: When our foundations are shaken in times of crisis, what are we left with? We are left with the frailty of fear, knowing that our self-made foundations are not strong enough even on our best day.

Nothing should replace our allegiance to Jesus Christ. Family and nation remain strong only when individuals within them have built their lives on a firm foundation, the rock of Jesus Christ. No other allegiance is as lasting as this one, and none other should take its place in our hearts.

When we don't give in to the fear of helplessness and fumble for control, we are able to take our rightful posture before God. We bow before Him on His throne, we rely on Him and depend on Him fully. And in being in His presence and soaking in His perfect love, all our fears will be cast out. When we do this, we are building our house on the rock—a sturdy foundation that will hold no matter what storms come our way.

WHO DO YOU TRUST WHEN YOU'RE AFRAID?

I grew up in Columbia, South Carolina. It was definitely out in the country—I guess you would call it "the country" since we lived on a dirt road. Across the dirt road was the woods, and beyond that a little lake that we visited often. One evening when I was in the fifth grade, Dad and I decided to watch the South Carolina sunset over the lake. We walked down the little path carved through the woods and we stood on the bank of this lake watching the sunset.

All of a sudden, Dad said, "Son, do you want to see a big water moccasin?"

I said, "Yes, sir, I do!"

"Look, Ed."

Right on the bank was a five-foot water moccasin—big, thick, muscular. This snake was so thick he had a goatee!

I said, "Wow, that's a big snake!" I looked to my right and said, "Dad, is that another one?"

Dad looked and said, "I think it is!" Then we saw another one and another.

I don't know what happened. I'm not sure if the water moccasins were in some kind of a mating frenzy, but we saw fifty water moccasins within a matter of minutes. They were on the bank, around our feet, in the water. I was terrified. I'll never forget what my dad said: "Son, jump on my back!"

I didn't have to take a running start. My vertical jump at that moment would have embarrassed an NBA all-star. I jumped on his back, grabbed him, and buried my face in his shirt. I'll never forget looking up and watching him with a flashlight as he navigated around all those snakes. He found the path and took us home. I knew Dad was in control of the situation. With him, I knew I was safe.

A lot of us right now are so fearful. We are in such turmoil, so apprehensive and anxious. Our heavenly Father is saying to us right now, "Trust me, I'm in control, I will get you through this and I will show you the way. You are safe with me. I know the way home."

It's one thing to trust God in times of plenty; we can sing worship songs about His goodness all day long. It's a completely different thing to trust God in times of lack, times of want, times of fear. In times like these, we all need the reminder that God is trustworthy.

Do you know what the word *trust* means? Our English word *trust* comes from an Indo-European root word meaning "to be solid," which is also the source of our word *tree*. If you want to be firmly planted, if you want to have deep roots, if you want your life to be solid, sturdy, and firm, then trust God. He is the only One who deserves our trust; He will never let us down. Placing your trust in yourself is like trusting in a daisy. When one of life's storms comes, your roots aren't going to be deep enough to remain planted. You will be uprooted and washed away. Only God is worthy of our trust.

One section of Scripture has been the theme Scripture for the Young family for generations. It's Proverbs 3:5-6: "Trust in the Lord with all your heart and do not lean on your own understanding; in all your ways acknowledge Him, and He will make your paths straight" (NASB).

When we lean on our own understanding, we are in trouble. We are powerless. We are like the man building his house on shaky foundations that can't withstand trials. Our own understanding is so easily plagued by fear. But when we lean on God's understanding—lean into His love—we are powerful. We are firm. We look at our fears through the lens of His love. What a message of hope.

We trust God by getting on our knees, naming our fears, taking our thoughts captive, and praying for His wisdom and guidance. God will navigate the snakes of life for us, we just have to trust Him and follow His guidance. When we pray, we are admitting our shortcomings and submitting to His will and control. Philippians 4:6 says: "Do not be anxious about anything, but in every situation, by prayer and petition, with thanksgiving, present your requests to God." Does this say just in tragedies? Does this say just in catastrophic things? Does this say when you are getting ready to close the big deal or undergo major surgery? No, it says, in *every* situation, pray. And then look what will happen: "And the *peace of God*, which transcends all understanding, will guard your hearts and your minds in Christ Jesus" (Philippians 4:7, emphasis added).

Everyone wants peace, don't they? We hear cries for civil, interracial, national, and international peace almost every day. But the peace that Paul speaks of here is more than that. Paul speaks of an inner peace for those who belong to Christ, for those who have been reconciled to God through His Son. If God's peace is going to "guard your hearts and your minds in Christ Jesus," then you must, first of all, be *in* Christ. If you want to have the peace of God, you must have peace *with* God. Our daily submission to Him through prayer is one way we can realign ourselves to His will and the work of His spirit.

Trusting in God is a daily decision. Throughout the

day, we can choose whether we are going to give in to fear and be enveloped by our feelings of helplessness, or we can name our fear, take our thought captive, readjust our posture, and trust. Choose to trust Him. When we surrender our fear of helplessness to God, we can replace it with trust in His sovereignty and control in our lives. When we ask God to shine His light in every room, closet, and attic of our heart and mind, He shows us that He is in control and we have nothing to fear. Let's invite Him to guide us as we face our fears and realize that all fear is no match for our great God!

CHAPTER 2

SCENARIO SICKNESS

FEAR OF THE FUTURE

When Lisa and I first started dating in high school, one of our favorite activities was to go fishing together. On one particular day, we ventured out to a familiar spot. We were pushing the boat off of the shore when I glanced down and saw a nest of about ten snakes under the boat. (I know what you're thinking: "This guy should stay away from lakes!" Not a chance, I love fishing too much!) Lisa didn't see them and was about to step into the nest with her next push of the boat. I grabbed her and "gently" pushed her out of danger to the side of the bank before attacking the snakes with the paddle. Needless to say, she was hysterical, I mean really hysterical! She was crying, screaming, and having a total meltdown while I was attempting to get the situation under control.

From that day forward, Lisa has had a huge fear of snakes and reptiles in general. As a young girl, she enjoyed the outdoors and finding bugs, snakes, and lizards. That enjoyment definitely ended on this day at the lake. This one experience has stayed with her for decades and continues to this day.

Most of us could share a similar story of a past experience that shapes our future fears. We allow a difficult or painful experience to follow us and haunt us in our daily lives. When we don't address our past traumas and invite God to heal us, we leave room for the fear virus to invade our lives and infect our thoughts with fear of the future.

Psalm 91:1-2 says "Whoever goes to the Lord for safety, whoever remains under the protection of the Almighty, can say to him, 'You are my defender and protector. You are my God; in you I trust'" (NIV).

That verse is talking about you and me. "Whoever" is "us" whenever we are willing to trust in God and His great plans for our lives despite our fears. Does this mean that bad things won't happen? Absolutely not! But does it mean that He'll use whatever happens for His glory and our good? Yes, undoubtedly! When we let our fear of the future invade our hearts and thoughts, we are not experiencing the full life that God has in store for us. When we trust fully in His plan and know that He'll work everything out for good, we can let go of our fears—fears that will keep us from dreaming. And our God has a significant history of fulfilling big dreams.

SCENARIO SICKNESS

We all deal with different fears. For many of us, it's the fear of the future, the fear of the unknown. The perceived consequences of these potentially unfavorable outcomes can feel very real.

This makes our fear feel very justified. We start asking "what if" questions: "What if I get sick? What if I don't pass the test? What if I don't make the team? What if I lose my job? What if they leave me? What if my child dies?" *What if this and what if that and what if . . .* We could ask these questions all day long.

I call that kind of questioning "scenario sickness," and that's something that we have to stay away from. How many of us can admit to playing out all these "what ifs" to the point where our imaginary fears make us sick? Scenario sickness feeds the process of "False Evidence Appearing Real," and it causes worry and fear to reign in our lives.

What's really stunning is the fact that 2,000 years ago, Jesus dealt with this very subject. He spoke about scenario sickness with a bunch of people sitting on a hillside during the Sermon on the Mount, the greatest sermon ever preached.

Jesus said these words in Matthew 6:25, "Do not worry about your life." If you look at the tense in Greek, it means, "stop worrying." Jesus is simply saying to all those people who were sitting in that amphitheater on the sea of Galilee, "Stop worrying. Yeah, you there, stop worrying. All of you who hear my voice now and for ages to come, stop worrying." And He is saying it you and me.

Later in verse 31 of Matthew 6, He talks about worry again, ". . . do not start worrying." He said to the worriers, "If you're worrying, stop. And if you're not worrying, don't start." Jesus is making it clear that worry has no place in our hearts. There is no healthy use for it now or in the future.

In Matthew 6:25, He tells us, "Therefore I tell you, do not

worry about your life, what you will eat or drink; or about your body, what you will wear. Is not life more than food and the body more than clothes?" What's He talking about? He's telling us not to worry about food, fitness, our bodies, our figures, getting "swole" all the time. Don't worry about fashion. (Wow, that's convicting to me!) And don't worry about finances. You can concern yourself with food, with staying in relatively good shape, with looking presentable with fashion, and with finance. But don't *worry* about it.

Dr. Robert Leahy, clinical psychologist and director of the American Institute for Cognitive Therapy in New York, reported a study that he did showing that 85 percent of what subjects worry about never happens. And with the 15 percent of events that did happen, most of the subjects discovered either they could handle the difficulty better than expected or they were grateful for a lesson learned through the experience. We take things from tomorrow and the next day and we dump it on today. That's why Jesus is saying to us, "Don't do it. You take care of what God has given you today and don't freak out about tomorrow."

When fear of the future and scenario sickness starts causing all the "what ifs" to pop into your head, remind yourself that Jesus is saying to you, "Don't worry about all of these 'what ifs' and fears of tomorrow, I've got you!"

WHAT ARE YOU FEEDING ON?

Often times, our "what ifs" are directly related to things that happened in our past that cause fear in our present. Our life experiences can set the course for our future fears if we tend to re-live things from our past. These things are not always very positive, and they can keep us down and cripple us in the future. The past is a tricky aspect of our lives that requires careful handling because it can either feed our hopes and dreams for the future or starve them. Dreams that we carry from our past feed us; fears that we carry from long ago keep us from being nourished in the present.

If we constantly remember the bad stuff from the past—the evil stuff, the traumas, the mistakes, the things done to us or the things we did to others—those things can freeze us in the present and hurt our prospects for the future. So, what can we do right now? We need to start by getting help outside of ourselves. Many of us should probably seek out a professional to help us process these traumas and the fears that they cause. We can also take some extremely healthy steps by just sharing the pain of our past with a trusted friend who is willing to listen.

We have all been there. You look back at yourself and remember the comment someone made about your personality or your looks. You focus on the many times you've messed up or made regrettable decisions in a relationship. You think to yourself, "Surely God can't use someone like me. He can't possibly make something positive out of all this." These kinds of thoughts reveal a fear of the future fed by fears from the past.

Could you be feeding off of the negative parts of your past and subsequently starving yourself of the future God has for you?

For instance, we all have been scarred by a bad meal. One of our family's favorite hobbies is dining out. We all enjoy going out to our favorite restaurants and dining as a family. On the rare occasion that we have a bad experience or the food is off, we will all remember it for a long time. We think twice before giving that restaurant a second chance because the experience sticks with us.

Painful memories can also stick with us, squelching our potential, feeding our fears, and leaving our dreams malnourished. This diet of fear and negative thoughts often comes from hurtful words or circumstances from childhood. If not processed properly, these negative memories from long ago creep into our consciousness over and over again until we succumb to their draining influence in our lives.

Psalm 34:8 says "Taste and see that the Lord is good." We need to feed on His words and His promises daily—sometimes minute by minute. They help us refocus on the lessons we have learned and remind us of God's provision and protection during the good times and the bad. Remember, you survived your past. Even during the darkest parts of your life, God was faithful to you. He didn't cause it, but He will use it to make you even stronger now as you face the fears ahead. God will use both the positive and negative experiences from the past to build us up and prepare us for a stronger future. But we must begin to have a daily diet of God's Word, talking to Him about our hurts and feeding on His love for us, and we will be able to stand firm—ready for anything.

STAND FIRM

The children of Israel often found it difficult to use the past in a positive way. Either they would distort the negative aspects of their bondage, and thereby discount their miraculous deliverance at God's hand, or they would forget all the good things God had done for them. Rather than looking at the past and having hope, they looked straight ahead and were filled with fear.

God miraculously delivered them from hundreds of years of slavery in Egypt. Through the ten plagues that eventually led to their freedom, He proved His power and glory time after time. After all that God had done for them, you would think they would look back and remember the supernatural acts of God from the past. When they found themselves pressed up against the Red Sea by the pursuing Egyptian army, it would make sense to hold onto the truth that God brought them out of slavery. You would expect them to trust God to deliver them once again from the hands of their enemies.

But the Israelites began to whine and complain because they were fearful. Instead of looking back and praising God for what He had done for them, they blamed God and Moses for putting them in another life-threatening predicament, for taking them away from their comfort zone of slavery and bringing them into the wilderness of new dangers.

They actually looked back at their slavery and oppression as a better and safer time. They were trapped by their past memories and their narrow perspectives. They wanted the security of their dysfunctional safety net. Imagine that! They we were actually longing for the chains of slavery! That's what fear does: it distorts the past and projects an unhopeful future.

They did not trust that following God into the unknown was better than the slavery they had previously known. They didn't believe that God could take those negative experiences and make something better out of their lives. In short, they were fearful of what lay ahead because it was out of their control. Their physical oppression led to oppressive thinking, and this mentality was all they knew. They were unwilling to move beyond the engrained emotions and memories that defined them.

This distorted view of the past led to fear and blame: "Oh, Moses, why did you bring us here? We were better off in slavery. We're better off the way we used to be. We never should have followed you!"

It is easy for us to look at the Israelites' circumstances and say, "That's unbelievable! How could these hardheaded people complain to the Almighty God? They need a major reality check." But we shouldn't be too critical of these stubborn Israelites because, in many ways, we are them.

When a world event wreaks havoc on the stock market or it radically disrupts our daily routines, many of us probably spend a good bit of time worrying about what will happen next. We wonder, "What will this mean for my family? What will this do to my future? When will we get back to normal?" Our wheels start coming off, and we let our worries dictate our responses. We get temporary amnesia about the evidence of

God's faithfulness in our lives. He has brought us through so much and proved to us so many times that we can stand firm in Him. And we can be confident that He will do it again!

Even if we fearfully spiral into scenario sickness again, the truth remains: God delivers His people again and again and again. We quickly lose sight of this truth in moments of panic, but as we look back through the lens of God's provision, we recognize that we are miraculously alive and still here breathing. So, take a deep breath. Seriously, think about what's weighing on you the most, and join me in taking a huge deep breath right now. Hold it in and release. God's got this.

He carried us through hard times before, and He'll carry us through hard times again. My prayer is that we learn this lesson quicker than Israel did.

In the midst of the Israelites' negative emotions, Moses stepped in and said, "Do not be afraid. Stand firm and you will see the deliverance the Lord will bring you today. The Egyptians you see today you will never see again. The Lord will fight for you; you need only to be still" (Exodus 14:13-14).

The beauty of Moses' words is that they are just as appropriate and beneficial to us today as they were back then. We need to remember them every time fear and negative emotions creep up. What an encouragement those words must have been to the people of Israel on that famous day in history. God's message of hope to you and me has not changed: "Do not be afraid, the Lord will fight for you!"

When you feel fear and uncertainty is overshadowing you, stand firm. The Bible says, "Be still, and know that I am God"

(Psalm 46:10). Do you feel like an Egyptian army is pursuing you? Do you feel pressed up against the Red Sea? Do you sometimes think to yourself, "I would be better off if things were the way they used to be," or "I've messed up too much for God to deliver me this time," or "If I trust again, I will just get hurt again"? It's time to be still and listen to the voice of God. Be ready to put one foot in front of the other as you prepare to follow God into the unknown.

TAKE THE NEXT STEP

Being still or standing firm doesn't mean we do nothing while we wait on God. Faith requires action. As we trust God with the future, we need to take the next step along the path. We need to step out of fear and into faith. Too many times, we are overwhelmed with the future because we try to see too far ahead; we want to figure out everything so there is no uncertainty. All God requires of us is to take the next step. We know that, ultimately, He holds the future in His hands. But He reveals only what we need to know, where we need to go, one step of faith at a time.

I use the calendar app on my phone a lot. If I push one of the numbers in those little boxes that make up the calendar, I'm told what's coming up this week, next week, or next month. Here's what I have discovered: I'm always best if I stay in that little box which says today's date. I really should not worry about the next day, the next week, or the next month. And when I stay in my box, I'll be in position to be led by God, to receive His blessings, and make the most of today. So, I need to say, "God, You're sovereign, You run my life today. I want to please You and glorify You." I will stay in my box today.

The problem comes when I look down the road and start taking all these boxes from the future and piling them onto myself today. I become a hoarder and I can't see over the stacks. I wall myself in and cannot clearly see what God wants me to do. Here's my dilemma: When I take boxes from the future—boxes of worry, boxes of fear, boxes I cannot control or influence—and put them on today, it will eventually break my back. Sadly, most of the boxes of tomorrow are complete fantasy and worse case "what if" scenarios.

Matthew 6:34 says, "Give your entire attention to what God is doing right now, and don't get worked up about what may or may not happen tomorrow" (MSG). Again, only 15 percent of what you fear and worry about is statistically even going to happen. God will be there to help you deal with whatever difficulties and challenges that you may face when the time comes. So many of us are weary, out of breath, and worn out because we're carrying boxes of things we're not even designed to carry. God is saying, "Don't worry about ten steps from now. Focus on the next step." Concentrate on what God is doing today, how He's strengthening you, how He's blessing you, the step He has for you, and He will prepare you for tomorrow in ways you could have never imagined!

Back to our Israelites. God continued speaking to Moses: "Tell the Israelites to move on. Raise your staff and stretch out your hand over the sea to divide the water so that the Israelites can go through the sea on dry ground" (Exodus 14:15-16). Before God even told Moses to raise his staff and divide the sea, He told the Israelites to "move on." God told them to move it when Moses had just told them to be still and stand firm. What are we to make of these seemingly contradictory orders?

First, Moses was addressing the people's inner turmoil when He told them to stand still. They were terrified, and they thought they had been brought to the desert to die. Fear had trapped their inner resolve and Moses was telling them to be at peace and remember that God would not let them down. He was telling them to still the conflicting thoughts in their minds, to let the peace of God permeate their hearts, and to know that God was still God. Nothing had changed as far as God was concerned; He had brought His people this far and was not going to let them die.

Moses' words were also a reaction to his people's desire to go backward instead of moving forward. The fight-or-flight mechanism was telling them to flee, to run back into the arms of their oppressors and beg for mercy. God had another plan. He was going to fight for them and take them forward to a land He had promised them, a land of freedom and opportunity. Moses was telling them to stand firm against their fear, not to take flight and run away from the obstacles before them.

God then said, "Move on," meaning just what it says: stop whining, get going, and trust Me. However, trust is not automatic, and God does not expect it to be. I have discovered in life that trust is a learned commodity, and we learn it best through the difficulties of life. God knows that and patiently works with us, but He does expect action. Like the Israelites, He wants us to move and take the next step in faith.

Think of it this way: it is easier for God to guide us when we are moving than when we are dead weight, standing still. Have you ever tried to move the steering wheel of a car that is not moving? The friction of the rubber against the pavement resists the guidance from the steering wheel. On the other hand, when the vehicle is in motion, you can steer the car with your pinkie finger. I wouldn't recommend this as a rule, but you can do it. Vehicles were designed to be steered on the go.

Likewise, people were created by God to be guided on the move as He often illuminates one step at a time. I wrote earlier of how Proverbs 3:5-6 has been a guiding verse for my family. It promises that God will make our paths straight if we trust Him one step at a time. Another one of my favorite passages in Scripture is Psalms 119:105, "Your word is a lamp to my feet, a light on my path." One reason I like this verse so much is the word picture it gives of walking along a path guided by a lamp or lantern. If you've ever done this, you know that a lantern does not provide much forward light. It illuminates the area right around you, providing enough light to see one or two steps ahead. If we focus on the darkness and the things we cannot see, fear will definitely consume us; but if we focus on the light and the next step, it will bring us peace.

This is a picture of someone who walks with the Lord. This is a person who trusts Christ to shine the light of His

Word just far enough for the next step. It would be easy if we had a detailed itinerary of future events. But He tells us just enough so we can trust Him with the future. We know the path will eventually take us home, but in the meantime, we have to follow the path each day just as far as God's light will show us.

BE BOLD

Instead of coming down with a case of scenario sickness, we can take another cue from the story of Moses. More specifically, let's look at a defining event in the life of Miriam, Moses' sister. Miriam was the oldest sister of Moses and she was bold, just like her younger brother. Her act of boldness changed history.

Before God freed the Israelites from slavery in Egypt, they were increasing greatly in numbers. They had grown as a people to such a degree that Pharaoh feared they would start an uprising against him. As a result, he gave an order that all male Hebrew infants must be thrown into the Nile River. It was during this time that Moses was born.

Moses' mother hid him for three months, but she could hide him no longer. Not wanting to drown him as the law required, she and her daughter Miriam made a floating bassinet, placed it in the river, and pushed him along the muddy waters of the Nile.

The Bible says that Miriam stood in the distance and watched as her brother Moses drifted downstream. She waited to make her move. I'm sure her heart was pounding and her mind was racing with all the fears and unknowns. The timing was perfect because Pharaoh's daughter was coming to the river to bathe. When Pharaoh's daughter took Moses out of the Nile and decided to keep him as her own, Miriam put her fears aside and walked up to her. "Have I got a deal for you! You need a nurse for the baby, and I know someone who would be perfect." Pharaoh's daughter ended up paying Moses' mother to take care of her own son, and the family was reunited.

Miriam did not give into scenario sickness. What if she had listened to all the possible horrible outcomes and fears that played in her mind over and over again? "Oh, what if I say the wrong thing to Pharaoh's daughter? What if she doesn't like my idea?" She didn't let those thoughts control her; she boldly went into the situation and did what she needed to do. God used Miriam to preserve Moses' life until he could fulfill his God-given destiny.

Miriam stepped out boldly and did not sit in bitterness of Pharaoh's decree. She believed that God would redeem the situation and save Moses. We do not know what might have happened to Israel if Miriam had been paralyzed by fear, if she had let the negative scenarios keep her from taking action at just the right time. God could have saved Moses by some other means, but only He knows what might have happened if Miriam had not stepped up to the challenge.

We have to realize that God has a plan for each of us. You may be thinking, "Ed, you don't know the pain of my past. God can't use me. You don't know the fear that I live with." You can't let pain from the past turn into fear of the future; you must boldly believe that God will redeem everything in His time. Only in living out our bold belief in God's redemption can we find true healing. When we let "what if" scenarios scare us away from fulfilling God's plan, there is no way to know how that will affect the future. We cannot know what chain of events will be set into motion by our lack of action. God's plan for mankind and His redemption will be accomplished regardless of how we act or react to the opportunities we are given, but in some mysterious way, God allows us to participate in His plan. And our action—or lack of action—somehow makes a difference in the quality of the outcome.

I will admit that there have been times over the years when I was hesitant to boldly believe in God's redemption and plan for me and for others. But as I look around at churches everywhere, I am so encouraged by the boldness and commitment of others to step out in faith. More importantly, as I look closer to home, my wife's boldness inspires me when she invites people to church or asks people she meets if she can pray for them. I have learned through watching others that when we partner with God in boldness, He will reach so many people and do incredible things through us.

Lisa and I met this couple who knew about Jesus but didn't really understand what it meant to have a relationship with Him. Lisa invited them to our Easter service, and despite our doubts, they showed up! They decided to keep coming and they both eventually took their understanding of who Jesus was from their head to their heart as they gave their lives to Christ!

It has been amazing to watch them grow in their relationship with Christ as they committed their family to making church a weekly priority. Now, they are boldly inviting so many people who don't know the Lord to experience Fellowship Church.

The husband recently told Lisa and me about how his extended family gives him grief over his faith and being a part of such a bold church that talks about our need for Jesus. But he continues to share with them about what God is doing in his life and hopes one day that they will have what he has. No one can deny that God is doing great things in this family's life.

He comes to our midweek gatherings and one week he told me, "Ed, I still can't believe I'm even coming to church in the middle of the week. I once thought, 'Why would I ever do that?'" Then he said, "You know what? When I go, I don't think about myself. I think about the people I am connecting with and how I can encourage and help them. You grow when you make it about others."

Here is a guy who was bold enough to admit that something was missing and started asking questions. He didn't give in to his fears; he humbled himself, sought out answers, and God redeemed his life. He realized his definition of Jesus was lacking and that he needed to go all in, so he boldly gave his life totally to Christ. Then he boldly took heat from his family and refused to let it keep him from growing and experiencing God's best for his life. He was also bold in his willingness to set aside time to serve and show love to others by inviting them and sharing his story with them. This is a guy who, like so many, could argue that he's too busy leading a large organization, spending time with his family, and enjoying his off time. Yet, he has made time for God to use him in the lives of others. It's beautiful to watch the impact faith is having on him, his marriage, his kids, and so many others who God is using him to reach.

What if we all prayed for an extra measure of boldness in living out our faith in Jesus? We might just be surprised to find that it is the very thing that drives fear out of our hearts. This man, just like Miriam, took a bold leap of faith and believed that God could redeem situations that seemed irredeemable. God is doing the impossible.

As we boldly step out, we grow stronger and more confident that we are following God's will, that He will redeem our past, and that He will help us carry out our work to completion. I say now, and have always said, that the ministry of Fellowship Church is a God thing. I pray that you can experience the joy of being a part of some incredible "God things" in your life as you step out boldly for Him.

God gives us the responsibility and the privilege of taking part in His work, and I have to believe that what we do makes a difference. God is sovereign, He is in control of everything, but we are also free beings with the capacity to make choices. And those choices affect the course of our lives and those of other people. Make the choice to be bold in your work for the Lord. Keep scenario sickness from striking by confessing negativism as sin and making bold moves for God as He leads you. Admit your fears, commit them to God, and prepare to take the next step of faith.

DECIDING TO DREAM

As we begin to make bold choices in our lives, we need to realize that life will be exciting. Sometimes it will seem beyond our control—and often it will be. But we don't need to fear the unknowns. God will be in control, and as the apostle Paul tells us, "His strength will be made perfect in our weakness" (2 Corinthians 12:9). Rest assured that life will always promise to be an exciting ride. Adventure and excitement are the essence of the Christian life.

There is nothing boring about being a Christian unless you are paralyzed by fear and take the easy road. But God has called us to the narrow road, filled with ups and downs, hills and valleys, and many tight curves and bends. This is the great adventure of following Christ, the roller coaster of a life of authentic faith. There is no place for worry or timidity in the kind of life God wants us to have. He calls us to dream big, and He promises to finish the good work He started in us (Philippians 1:6).

As we begin to release control and live fully the life God has for us, we will see joy cut through the fear. Sometimes, even in the midst of painful or stressful times, we are given the gift of simple joys in the little things of life. You watch as your child plays without a care in the world. The sun shines after a long rain. A moment of laughter breaks out as you share a great a meal with a friend. You hear the words "I love you" at just the right time from someone you cherish. Through the gifts of these joys, you begin to realize that tomorrow has enough problems of its own and the past is the past, so it is all right to enjoy God's gift of today.

Now let's do a quick inventory. Are you infected with scenario sickness? If you are, break away from the "what ifs" and say, "God, I want be bold and strong. I want to be surrounded by people who challenge me to be bold and strong. Help me let go of my 'what ifs' and replace them with an assurance of Your plans and purposes for my life. Amen!"

In Matthew 6:34, Jesus said, "Do not worry about tomorrow; it will have enough worries of its own." The word worry literally means to be pulled in different directions. Are you being pulled in different directions? It's time to commit to going in one direction.

God knows your tomorrows. When you yield to His control and trust the future to Him, you have found the antidote for future fears. Instead of being pulled in different directions, allow yourself to be led in only one direction—God's direction. Stand firm, dream big, take the next step, be bold, and commit to His path for your life!

CHAPTER 3

FINISH THE RACE

FEAR OF COMMITMENT

There is nothing like the moment when a doctor is telling you that your child has an incurable diagnosis. Our son, EJ, was born with a neurological disease called neurofibromatosis. For those of you who don't know what that is—I certainly didn't when I first heard it—it's a disease where tumors grow on the nerve endings. Throughout his early life, he had testing at least every other year at M.D. Anderson Hospital in Houston.

When he was growing up, you would have thought he was a completely normal and healthy kid. However, physically and developmentally, he was always about three years behind other kids. For example, if you said, "EJ, run over here," the first three or four steps he would look normal. But after about the fourth or fifth step, his stride would just break down. Or, if you had him shuffle from side to side, he could do it a few times, but he couldn't maintain his momentum and coordination after that.

EJ didn't really play organized sports, but when he was sixteen, he said, "Mom and Dad, I'm going to try out for the track team." I thought to myself, "Track team? How is he going to do that?" But I said to him, "Really? . . . That's great!" Then he explained why: "You know, Mom and Dad, the great thing about the track team is they don't cut anybody." This was going to take a tremendous amount of effort and commitment on EJ's part with very little guarantee of success due to his physical challenges.

The first track meet that he competed in was a huge event. A thousand people were in the stands from all of the schools in the area. We asked, "EJ what event are you going to run?" He said, "The hundred-meter dash." And I thought, "That's the race for the strongest and fastest of runners." I was proud of his courage, but I was also concerned for him. So, Lisa and I showed up at the track meet, and all these heats are going on. Finally, it comes to EJ's heat and the announcers call out his name. When we heard his name, (parents, you can understand this!), we just broke down in tears. I mean, the emotions and memories of all the testing, all of the praying, all of the meeting with doctors just welled up inside of us, and we were basket cases.

All of the sudden, "Bang!" the crack of the starting gun. All these kids take off, and the crowd begins to cheer. No exaggeration, the runners are at fifty meters and EJ is maybe at ten meters. The runners crossed the finish line, and everyone thought the race was over. The cheering died down. All of a sudden, I saw some people turn and look at my son and the applause started. It grew bigger and bigger until it was a full out standing ovation.

The other runners had already crossed the finish line, but I had never seen EJ run this well. He was running the race of his life. He was fearless and finally crossed the finish line to great celebration from the crowd. Lisa and I watched him through the tears. He held his head up. He was congratulating the other runners and celebrating with his teammates. And I thought, "I could not do what he just did. I don't have that kind of stuff in me."

EJ is now a young married man with an absolutely amazing wife, Jess. He has a great heart for God and is just an outstanding young man. And as I've reflected back on that story, I have asked myself this question: "Who ran the best race that afternoon: those muscular kids, those guys who could just fly, or my son?" There's no doubt about it: my son. The tests he had to consistently take, the work he had to go through, and the training he had to endure in a body that would not cooperate with him. He committed himself, no matter the cost. There was no other option but to courageously finish the race.

In our world today, what EJ did is very uncommon. We'd rather bail out than blast through. If it doesn't come naturally, then we drop it. We'd rather leave than last. We'd rather throw in the towel than stay in the game. It's so easy to waver and waffle and take the path of least resistance. Why? Because we fear this ten-letter word that symbolizes accountability, integrity, and discipline: commitment.

From month-to-month apartment leases to prenuptial agreements, from playing career hopscotch to escape clauses, our culture is characterized by a lack of or fear of commitment.

"I don't want to be hemmed in," we declare. "I want to keep my options open. I don't want to be stifled or handcuffed." Commitment means pledging yourself to a position no matter the price tag, pledging yourself to a stance no matter what the cost. It's intimidating, but if you make the effort to invest in commitment, the returns will be awesome.

Too often, we are fair-weather fans of the game of life. Things are going well for us. We're making money, the stock market is up, the marriage is going well. Our relationships are just sailing along, and we look committed. Then we get a couple of losses under our belt, there's a pandemic, the economy goes south, we lose our number one client, we have a conflict. When that happens, we seek the fastest exit. Because we are not really committed for the long haul, a few setbacks threaten to derail us.

It's really important to understand how the fear virus affects our relationships and commitment quotient. Some of us fear commitment because we've been rejected. We have put our heart and soul into something and had it trashed, so we are apprehensive about putting it out there again. The fear virus starts infecting our thoughts, saying "You're better off alone. No one can hurt you this way." Others of us have had an authority figure—perhaps a parent or teacher or coach—commit to us and then fall through on their promise. Maybe they said they were going to show up, take us to the game or fishing or shopping, and they didn't keep their word. We remember the hurt of those experiences and fear going through the same thing again. Yet another group of us fears commitment because we have broken promises ourselves. We don't like to dwell on those failures, so we say, "Why think about it? Why talk about it? Why make commitments if I can't ever follow through on the promises I make?"

All of these things lead to a fear of commitment, but our true fear can be traced all the way back to the soil of the Garden of Eden. The Bible says that God was committed to Adam and Eve. He showed His hand; He put His cards on the table. Adam and Eve recognized this, and in turn, they were committed to God. When God said, "Adam, Eve, don't touch the fruit of the tree in the middle of the garden," they responded with, "Lord, we are committed to that. We want to obey you. We want to follow you. We want to be your people."

Satan always attacks our commitment and tries to infect us with the fear virus whenever possible. If you do a quick background check on him, you'll discover that he always struggled with commitment himself. When he was in heaven as Lucifer, he struggled with staying committed to God and got kicked out. From that day forward, he has been trying to tear apart your commitment and mine. So Satan attacked Adam and Eve. He said, "Hey, guys, God is holding out on you. If you eat of the fruit of the tree, you will become like God. Don't really commit to Him. For once, just back off. For once, just bail out. For once, just leave." Adam and Eve tried it. They blew their commitment and failed the test, and from that day forward, we have been struggling with this issue.

Psalm 37:5 reads, "Commit your way to the Lord, Trust also in Him, and He will do it" (NASB). What a promise and an assurance! And 1 Kings 8:61 tells us, "May your hearts be fully committed to the Lord our God, to live by his decrees and obey his commands, as at this time." Notice the phrase "at this time." Now is the only time you have for sure to commit. Yesterday is gone and tomorrow is uncertain. You can't bring back any other time in your life, but you can commit yourself to God right now, today.

In every relationship, we must face the decision of commitment. Whether in marriage, in dating relationships, in your relationship with your kids, your friendships, or your mentorships, you will find yourself at the crossroads of commitment. When the fear starts bubbling up, you must decide and prepare for commitment to where God is leading you and the values that He calls you to.

SHIFT INTO FOUR-WHEEL DRIVE

Many individuals fear commitment in some of the most important areas of life. For example, commitment in your faith, in your career, in dating, in friendships, in parenting and in your marriage—these are just a few areas where fear can sabotage our ultimate commitments.

Let's talk about marriage, for instance. Marriage is wonderful, the most important earthly relationship we will ever have. But I would be lying to you if I said that marriage was a cruise-control situation. I used to drive a pickup truck with four-wheel drive. I didn't use the four-wheel drive feature very much, but now and then it helped me out. I knew that if I got into an off-road situation, I could shift into four-wheel drive to get out.

If you are married, you have off-road moments. Moments where you fear that you won't make it through, seasons that feel like you're holding on by a thread. When these off-roading moments happen, under the weight of the pressure, you fear that these rocky times won't end and you start looking for an exit. This is when the fear of commitment strikes, not during the honeymoon stage when the road is smooth but when the road disappears and you're not sure where to go. You can't just cruise down the road at full speed and expect to never encounter bumps along the way.

You have to slow down from time to time or pull aside and take an off-road detour.

Lisa and I have had our off-road moments, days, weeks, and years. We had them in the past, and we will have them in the future. When you hit a sticking point and you have a problem, it is as though you've suddenly veered off the smooth freeway and started off-roading. Mud is slinging; you are burning up fuel. But if you are committed, totally committed, if you have pledged yourself to a position no matter what, you will shift into four-wheel drive and get through the situation. You will burst through it and build deeper levels of commitment, love, and intimacy.

There will always be temptation to look for an exit because of fear, but you must resist that temptation and fight against your fear and choose to commit. Sometimes when husbands and wives hit some off-road situations or when it gets a little dicey and the vehicle starts to spin, they just bail out. They ditch the car and say, "I'm going to find another one. I need to get into another relationship, another marriage." Little do they realize that they will hit the same off-road patches in the next marriage, and the next, and the next. If you are not willing to four-wheel drive it, then, to put it bluntly, do not get married. Trust me, it will save you a lot of pain and heartache if you will assess your level of commitment now and back off. This is better than getting into the thick of the relationship and realizing that you never had the commitment level you needed to stick it out, to commit for the long haul.

What separates great marriages from mediocre ones? Great marriages are willing to go through the off-road times because both partners know it is worth it when they do it God's way. Sadly, most husbands and wives wait too long to say one little word that can change the course of their marriage: *Help!* When they feel stuck and the wheels are spinning, instead of saying "Help!", they just sit there in their fear and resign themselves to being stuck. Getting help looks like seeking a great Christian friend, a pastor, or a Christian counselor who could help them get unstuck and navigate the off-road seasons.

If you were driving home from work and you had some car trouble, would you just sit there in the middle of the road for a couple of years? No, you'd get proactive. You would get on your phone and do something. If you are in a marriage relationship that is stuck in the mud with your tires spinning, don't just sit there; do something. Get help. Be committed and say, "We're going to work it out. We're going to make it happen. We're going to do it God's way."

You also have to be willing to shift into four-wheel drive with your children. Moms and dads these days say, "We want to bring up kids who are committed." Parents say that, yet they go back on their word. They sign up but don't show up. Parents expect their children to be committed, but parents need to know that children learn their commitment cues from the committed behavior—not just the words—of Mom and Dad. They are taking it all in, watching us. We are always on stage in the family theater, and the spotlight never grows dim.

Be committed to spending time with your children, both quantity time and quality time. You may rationalize the lack of time you spend with your children by saying, "I may not have a lot of time to give, but I spend quality time with my kids." That's a fallacy. Kids do not understand this concept, and, quite frankly, it is just an excuse to make parents feel better about their misplaced priorities and lack of commitment. Quality time emerges from quantity time. Those special moments emerge spontaneously from spending time—large quantities of time—with them.

This commitment to our children includes quality conversation. It means really listening to them, even when the content of their conversation seems trivial to us. It's not trivial to them. Make eye contact with them and communicate that their presence is important to you. If you listen to them when they are five, they will talk to you when they are fifteen and twenty-five.

Make sure, moms and dads, that the most important thing you are committed to in your relationship with your child is introducing them to an intimate and vibrant relationship with the Lord Jesus Christ. That starts with you modeling your own commitment to Christ by having a healthy marriage (I didn't say perfect). I am talking about a marriage that places your spouse first and your kids second. Then together, you have the great opportunity to teach them how to pray and how to read the Bible. Make sure you make church as a family a weekly priority. Find a local church that offers age-appropriate teaching for preschoolers, children, and students. Your kids will often push against going to church. It's completely normal as they will test boundaries, but it should not keep you from taking charge and doing what you know is the right thing for the spiritual welfare of your children. They may say, "I don't want to go. It's not my thing. None of my friends will be there." You know, it might be a growing experience that their regular friends are not there. They will make new friends from families that are also committed to making church a priority in their lives. Parents, this is an off-road stretch where you need to shift into four-wheel drive. I want to ask you a basic question: Who is in the driver's seat? Are you driving, or have you given your children the keys?

I grew up in a family where my parents had the keys and held tightly to the steering wheel. My mom and dad were not perfect, but their commitment to each other and to raising each of their kids to have a committed relationship with God will always stand out more than any fault or parenting faux pas. All of their kids stayed the course because my parents were willing to four-wheel drive it. They would listen when I complained about going to church and respond, "Ed, we appreciate that. We hear you, but jump in the car, baby, because we're going to church today."

Church has always been a focal point in our family's life. More than that, we were raised in a home that took Christian commitment seriously. Our commitment to the local church was an outgrowth of our commitment to living out biblical principles individually and as a family unit. Christianity is not a one-day proposition. It is a full-time, full-out commitment to the person and teachings of Jesus Christ. Do your family priorities reflect that kind of commitment and dedication to following Christ? All of these commitments are worth fighting for, and with the power of God, you will be successful in overcoming your fears.

THE BIMBA PRINCIPLE

When I think of our family priorities and making God the center of family life, I can't help but mention the apostle Paul's warning in 2 Corinthians about being unequally yoked. If both partners are not committed to the things of God growing out of a vibrant relationship with Jesus Christ, then trying to make Christ the center of family life will be even more of an uphill struggle than it already is.

So, let me warn you now, if you are a Christian single

contemplating a marriage relationship with an unbeliever, you are in for some serious heartache and misery. Just do not go there. I can't say it more forcefully than that. God has given us this warning because of the kind of struggles that will inevitably follow if you try to build a marriage and family with an unbelieving spouse. You end up settling for someone who does not have the same priorities and values because of your fear of being alone.

I have some friends who live in Cancun, Mexico. I visited them years ago, and they had a pet monkey named Bimba that really took a liking to me. Monkeys are strong and have a tenacious grip. Bimba would hold on to me all day and let me carry her around everywhere. But if I wanted to put her down, she would dig in her nails and wrap her tail around me. Bimba was going to hold on to me no matter what.

Singles, you have to remember the Bimba principle: Hold on tight to God's teaching concerning spouse selection. Don't let go of one very important principle from Scripture that speaks directly to choosing your life partner because God gives this to us for our own good. Paul says in 2 Corinthians 6:14, "Do not be bound together with unbelievers; for what partnership have righteousness and lawlessness, or what fellowship has light with darkness?" (NASB).

What's going on here? Is God being discriminatory? No. Is God saying that we should never have friends outside the family of God? No. Is He insisting that our best friends and the people we date have the same spiritual intensity we do? Emphatically, yes! He is saying that the people we are closest to must share the same treasure that we share.

Why would God say this, specifically in the dating area? When you are dating, you are really thinking about finding a mate. I don't care how casual the date is; you are thinking about getting married. Could this be the one? Could this be him? Could this be her? God insists on this rule because He wants us to share ultimate intimacy. He knows how terrible it would be for us to be entwined with someone who we couldn't share the most important thing in our life. I have talked to many, many couples where one is a Christ-follower and the other is not. They are going in different directions. One partner is tapping into God's source, and the other is tapping into something else. In short, they have some serious problems with focus and priorities in their marriage and family.

God also wants us to have spiritual compatibility because of the challenges of childrearing. If we share Him, we will operate from the same foundation, the same authority, and the same absolutes when we are rearing children. Both parents will be unified in saying, "Hey, we are going to church. You are going to the junior high or high school ministry." If one parent is urging the child to think of the things of God and the other is saying, "Come on, honey, it doesn't matter; just let the kid do what he wants," you are in for a lot of pain and anguish.

Single women, in particular, tend to go through an interesting transition. When they are young, they say, "OK, I am going to commit to the Bimba principle. I am going to hold on. I'm going to do it God's way." Then one day, they suddenly realize that the biological clock is ticking, and they begin to change. Their standard of finding and marrying a man who is committed to Christ and His principles degenerates into, "Well, if he shaves and wears pants, that is good enough for me. I can change him; I can tweak him. He'll come around eventually." Let me caution you not to let your fear of being single forever compromise God's absolute best for you.

If you are a single man reading this and laughing, hold on. Don't laugh too soon, because men aren't any better in the realm of commitment than women. Here are what guys tend to do when faced with commitment. Too many Christian guys get right on the edge of a committed relationship and bail out. They have a good relationship with a Christian girl, and they know that pretty soon they are going to have to take the next step. But they freak out and let fear take over: "Wow, if I got married, I would have to be responsible! I couldn't play in thirteen softball leagues at once! I know she loves the Lord, but what if I meet a supermodel who loves Jesus."

Guys, we are pretty stupid. It's important to be attracted to the person you date and the person you marry. But if you always say, "Well, I'm waiting for someone better-looking," you will never get anywhere. God wants you to look as He does: first at the heart, not the body. Obviously, first you are attracted to someone, but marriage is a step of faith, a step of commitment to that one person with whom you can partner in service to the Lord for life. Outward beauty will fade, and the body will begin to give way, but the spiritual strength of your relationship will last forever.

The bottom line is that you have to pledge yourself to a position and hold on for dear life, no matter what. And the first commitment should be to determine to follow God's principle of marrying a like-minded follower of Christ. Don't let your emotions or your lusts win the day on this one.

If you are currently in a dating relationship in which you have doubts about the other person's commitment to Christ, take a step back to allow God to give you discernment. See a counselor or maybe read *Fifty Shades of THEY*, a book that I wrote about intentionally seeking relationships with people that are Tough, Honest, Encouraging, and Yielded to God. Seek out help that will give you more insight into God's principles about dating and marriage. Marriage is a lifelong commitment, so be sure you are with someone with whom you can also share your number one commitment. And when the right person comes along, fight against your fear of commitment and pledge yourself fully to that person.

RELATIONSHIP OR RE-LEACH-IONSHIP?

Let's take it a step further: from marriage and parenting, to dating, and now to friendships. Just about anyone you ask these days will tell you that close friends are hard to find and even harder to keep. You may be surrounded by people at work, at church, and in the neighborhood, but maybe you don't really have any committed friends.

It would be nice to say that the problem lies with everyone

else, but I'm afraid we will have to spread the blame around evenly. As we examine the reasons for a lack of committed friendships in our lives, we need to look first at ourselves for answers to the problem. Why can't we commit to our friends? What is the problem?

We may blame our addiction to our phones, or the large size of our churches, or our busy schedules, but those really are just surface issues. The problem, I believe, stems from a fear of committing to a few solid friendships. We spread ourselves thin with pseudo-deep friendships that ultimately leave us drained. There is a lack of balance in the way we cultivate and maintain relationships.

Instead of real, mutual friendships, a lot of us have people we frequently hang out with who drain us and leave us dry. We need to assess our relationships and see with whom we can cultivate life-giving, authentic friendships. So, when you think of your friends, are they healthy relationships or are they "re-leach-ionships"? Like a leach, do you have so called friends that drain the life out of you?

"Re-leach-ionships" take what they need without regard for what you need. I don't mean to be unkind or uncharitable, but there are people out there who, if we are not careful, will take and take and take and never give back. These are people who constantly come to us for counsel, who want to spend a lot of time with us so they can download all of their troubles, and who may even want financial or other help from time to time. But when you leave their company, you feel wiped out. They have become more of a ministry to you than a nourishing friendship. Because of negative experiences like these, we often shy away from committing to close relationships with people who really care about us.

Let me be clear. There is most certainly a place for people like that in our lives. We are called by Christ to minister to the needy, to help people, and give to people in the name of Christ, but we must also have mutually uplifting and encouraging relationships with people who give as much to us as we give to them. When you surround yourself with "re-leach-ionships," you won't have enough energy left over to get into good, replenishing relationships—the kind of solid relationships that hold you accountable, challenge you, and encourage you.

Even if we know we need to, it can be difficult to distance ourselves from these "re-leach-ionships." I'm not saying you have to tell them, "Forget you," and never speak to them again. I'm just suggesting that you should turn down the intensity of those relationships that zap your strength, and build up the intensity of replenishing, refueling relationships. You must have a balance of both. If you are too tired to even begin seeking friends who will nourish you, then you are out of balance. I encourage you to distance yourself from the relationships that are draining you.

You must seek out and cultivate friendships on a regular basis that will give you the energy and the strength to carry out the opportunities God gives you. You simply cannot pour into others, always giving of yourself, without being recharged. In order to cultivate these friendships, you have to overcome your fear of being vulnerable and choose to be yourself around these people.

How can you tell the difference between a healthy relationship and a "re-leach-ionship"? If you are with friends and you find yourself looking at your watch and saying, "Whoa, is it midnight already? I can't believe how fast the time goes by," that's a life-giving friendship. If you are sharing with them what really makes you tick—your dreams and hopes and fears—and they are doing the same with you, those are replenishing relationships. If you leave them feeling energized and ready to face the world, those are nourishing relationships. And, obviously, the people you call your closest friends should know Christ personally and have the same desire to please Him as you do. When you have friends like that, you will soar. Your commitment quotient will increase, and you will have an incredible return on your relational investment.

In "re-leach-ionships," on the other hand, you find yourself looking at your watch and saying, "Has it only been thirty minutes? It feels like I've been talking to this guy for hours." You'll be giving away more than you receive because these types of relationships are one-sided. You minister to them, but they have little or nothing to offer you.

Again, there is a place for these relationships because Christ had relationships like these. Jesus was often so drained by those to whom He ministered that He had to draw away from the crowds and spend time alone with the Father, the ultimate replenishing relationship. Luke records one such experience: "Yet the news about Him spread all the more, so that crowds of people came to hear Him and to be healed of their sicknesses. But Jesus often withdrew to lonely places and prayed" (Luke 5:15-16). Jesus also spent a lot of time with His disciples, the Twelve with whom He had chosen to interact and share His life. He would draw away with them, pray with them, and they would draw strength from one another (see Mark 6:31).

Jesus found balance between friendship relationships and ministry relationships because He was attuned to when He needed to seek refuge in the arms of the Father or those other select few who recharged Him for continued ministry.

Don't discount the power of friendship in shaping your life as you grow in the Lord and serve Him. With nourishing friendships, you can find the strength and the courage to tackle fear and live a godly life. Yes, God does often give us the strength to tread the waters of bold faith when no one else stands with us. But even the greatest men of faith in the Scriptures had strong companions who stood by them. David and Jonathan, Paul and Timothy, Moses and Aaron, Joshua and Caleb, Jesus and His disciples—these are all examples of committed friends who stood by one another, replenished one another, and served God more effectively together. We need the encouragement and support of committed Christian friends. And we need to be willing to serve in that same capacity for others. Push past your fear, assess your friendships, and get vulnerable.

A SECOND CHANCE

You might be saying, "Well, Ed, this is interesting. I understand what you're saying, but Ed, you don't know me. I have messed up on so many commitments. I have broken promises to my spouse, my children, my friends, and my life has suffered. Is there a chance for me? Can I start afresh, start anew today?"

I can think of no better way to answer that question than by taking a page out of the life of Simon Peter, one of Jesus' most beloved disciples. On the night Jesus was betrayed, Simon Peter said these words to Jesus: "I will lay down my life for you." Then Jesus answered, "Will you really lay down your life for me? I tell you the truth, before the rooster crows, you will disown me three times!" (John 13:37-38). Peter said he was committed, but Jesus knew the deep-seated fear in Peter's heart. When times would get tough, when Peter's world would begin to unravel upon the arrest of Jesus, and the doubts would creep in, Jesus knew the potential for weakness and disloyalty even before Peter did.

Jesus was arrested, taken to the house of Caiaphas, and thrown into a dungeon. Simon Peter trailed along to see what happened and started warming himself by a fire outside. Three times people asked him if he knew Jesus, if he associated with Him. Peter was afraid they would arrest him too—he had the fear of commitment and the hardship it could bring—so three times he denied his relationship with Jesus. He even started cursing.

Jesus was crucified and buried. Simon Peter, the man who

failed in his commitment to Jesus, went back to fishing. It was all he knew. Nothing seemed to make sense anymore, so he returned to the one thing in his life that had always made sense: being a fisherman.

Jesus rose from the dead and appeared on the shore of the Sea of Galilee where Simon Peter was fishing. The sun was just coming up; it was that time of morning when your eyes can play tricks on you. John 21 records an exchange between Jesus and these fishermen who did not recognize Jesus at first. Jesus yelled out to them (I am paraphrasing), "Hey guys, caught anything?" The fishermen replied, "No, we've fished all night and got nothing." Then Jesus said, "Throw your nets on the right side."

They did what He said, and there were so many fish they could barely pull the net up. When Peter felt the size and weight of this catch, he just dove in and swam to shore. He knew something was up. Then he saw Jesus standing by a fire making breakfast. When Peter saw that fire, he must have thought about the night by the fire when he disowned Jesus three times, how he had blown it, how he had come up short in his commitment to his Lord.

What did Jesus do? What He does with all of us when we fail. Jesus reinstated him, forgave him, and empowered him. He addressed Peter's fears and He called him back to commitment with a simple question: "Do you love me?" Three times Jesus asked Peter this question: "The third time he said to him, 'Simon son of John, do you love me?' Peter was hurt because Jesus asked him the third time, 'Do you love me?' He said, 'Lord, you know all things; you know that I love you.'

Jesus said, 'Feed my sheep'" (John 21:17).

Yes, it hurt a little to be asked the same question three times, but Christ asked it not for His own sake but for Peter's. Peter had denied Him three times, and he needed to be reassured of his own commitment to Christ in the same manner as he had disowned Him. Christ knew Peter loved Him, but He wanted to make sure that Peter knew himself that he loved Christ. And the mark of his love was the commitment to love and care for Jesus' sheep, the people of God who would also be called to follow the Good Shepherd.

Simon Peter emerged from being reinstated by Christ as one of the most committed men ever to live. It doesn't matter what you have done or how many times you've blown it—there is no way we will ever blow it like Simon Peter did, and look what happened to him. There is another chance for you, another day for you. You can become a man or woman of great commitment because Christ is ultimately, irrevocably committed to you.

Despite humanity's dismal performance on the playing field of life, Jesus Christ demonstrated the ultimate act of commitment toward us: "While we were still sinners, Christ died for us" (Romans 5:8). We were not worthy of it, but He paid the ultimate fine for your sins and mine. While Jesus was gasping for air, His lungs collapsing under His own weight, Satan was probably whispering in His ear, "Bail out. Throw in the towel. Don't finish the race." But Jesus was committed and pledged Himself to a position, no matter the price—even when the price was death.

He overcame any fear He had and committed Himself completely to us. Now He's waiting for us to do the same—no reservations.

Can you imagine how proud our heavenly Father is as He is watching us run our race? Can you imagine the standing ovation in heaven as you let go of your fear and commit to run His way? He is not asking you to be the strongest or run the fastest. He is asking you to keep running through the fear and hurdle those commitment barriers. Let nothing stop you and finish strong.

CHAPTER 4

MAY CAUSE
PARALYSIS

FEAR OF FAILURE

Most of us are familiar with taking a photo, scrolling through to find the perfect shot, doing a little editing and posting it. When it comes to the fear of failure, we tend to look at others and take a mental snapshot of their most successful moments, their new promotion and perks, their spectacular family vacation, beautiful or handsome spouse and kids, and we think to ourselves, "Must be nice." We start questioning, "What's wrong with me? Why I am I such a failure compared to them?" What we don't see in this snapshot is the years of struggle, setbacks, and secret suffering that most everyone goes through.

You can't take just one "perfect picture" of Lisa and me, our family, and Fellowship Church and know the whole story. You can't look at the great kids, grandchildren, multiple church locations, a camp and retreat center, our television program that reaches around the world, and just look at that and say to yourself, "I know the whole story." And I can't do that when I look at you. There's no way with one photo that anyone could capture every breakthrough and every breaking point. You won't see when Lisa and I were first married with a broken-down house or when we drove to Dallas with one car, one kid, and one dog to start Fellowship Church with thirty families in a little office complex. We had left one of the largest churches in America, where my dad was the pastor, a place of security and comfort. You don't see the people who bolted when the going got tough, when people said they loved us and were with us no matter what—until they weren't.

Lisa and I knew that failure was a real possibility. I was well aware that most church plants die after their first few years. You might say failure was even a probability for us. Even when we started to experience success and some recognition, it came with opposition and almost a story-ending disaster. Eight years into Fellowship Church, we had a trusted friend and staff member who completely betrayed us and lied to our church. He completely deceived us about a multimillion-dollar donation with layers of supporting documentation, bank records, and backstory for reasons that we still don't understand. What we do know is that by the time we figured it out, we had already bought our first piece of land for a permanent location for Fellowship Church and began building. With thousands of people meeting in rented facilities, it was time to find a place we could call home. We had increased the size and scope of our children's ministry areas and nearly doubled the size our worship center because of the promise of those funds. The dream of Fellowship

Church hung in the balance when one day I pressed this guy to "show me the money," and after hours on the phone, he finally admitted to me that he lied about everything. I hung up the phone, and I completely believed Fellowship Church was over that very moment. What a run it had been. That fear of failure I had kept at a distance finally caught up with me and consumed my heart and mind.

Fellowship Church was going to be a failure, a total loss. So many families were going to be hurt, and so many in the future would not be reached. I was literally on my knees processing this colossal failure. However, I thank the Lord I married a woman like Lisa, because she said, "Honey, God has called us to build His church. If it's not here, it's going to be somewhere else. He will give us the strength; He will give us the power to do it." Isn't that incredible? Did I marry out of my league or what? So, we took it one day at a time and worked through the fear, fought for the vision that God had given us, and were faithful to Him even though many times we didn't feel like fighting for it.

At the time, it was not a pretty picture. But now looking back, this failure is a part of the beautiful story of God's faithfulness to us as we faced our fear and shortcomings. He provided for us and protected us in ways we could have never imagined. And I have no doubts that God desires to do the same for you! So, let's crash through some quitting points together. As long as you are still in the fight and willing to take the next faithful step, you are not a failure. You are an incredible and beautiful story of God's faithfulness getting ready to happen!

Fear of failure arguably causes the biggest blockage in our

hearts. It can keep us from what God has for us, it can make us stagnant in our faith, our relationships, our careers, and our goals. When the fear virus attacks our hearts and starts whispering about failure, we have to fight back. We must remember that God is with us, guiding us, helping us finish the work that He started in us. God is a God of victory. He never lets it end with failure if we turn to Him; He always redeems, always loves, always lifts us up. Undoubtedly, you have some dreams that have not been realized, and we have to ask ourselves: What is the blockage? What is holding you back?

WHAT'S HOLDING YOU BACK?

In the life of every person alive today, certain things are brooding just beneath the surface. We keep them closely hidden, under wraps, buried deep inside of us. These things don't often show themselves because they are suppressed and held at bay by our own fears. Many people spend a lifetime ignoring these subsurface dwellers, confining them to the deep, dark recesses of their minds and hearts, never to be seen again.

What are these mysterious things lurking deep inside each one of us? They are our dreams of accomplishment and success. I am talking about the hopes, plans, and aspirations we have for our lives—the things we would tackle today if we knew we would succeed. I have never met anyone who does not have these kinds of dreams. Some people keep them hidden more than others, but they are there. A rare few are fulfilling their dreams. They have taken risks in life that not many are willing to take to achieve the deep-seated longings in their hearts.

If you are one of those rare people, you may not need to read this chapter. You have my permission to just skip it. But for the rest of us, I have a few simple questions: What's holding us back? What is keeping us from achieving those things that we know will make our lives more fulfilling? Why are we so hesitant to embark on those journeys, to try those things which will give us the deep satisfaction of accomplishment and success? What is holding our skill sets, our gifts, and our God-given talents at bay?

I believe the answer is fear. Specifically, we have paralyzed our own hopes and dreams by our own fear of failure. We are afraid of trying something and messing up, of making an attempt just to fall flat on our faces. We are afraid of taking risks and the hard work it would take to achieve success. We have become so comfortable in our mediocre existence, not trying, not taking risks, and not stepping out. We opt for the security of the familiar rather than the risk of the unfamiliar. We might be thinking, "What if I fulfill those dreams and they are not what I expected them to be? What happens after I achieve that goal? What do I do next?"

The word *failure* sounds so defeating, so depressing. But we have several choices in the face of failure—and, I assure you, everyone fails at some time or another in life. Here are our choices when we fail: we can deny it, dwell on it, blame others for it, or we can allow it to mature and develop us. Only the last option gives us the strength and the courage to go on and to move toward achieving our goals.

One of the main reasons we all struggle with this fear of failure is that we have a skewed view of success. We don't understand what success is all about. As far as our culture is concerned, success is more or less relative. A successful meal prepared in one of our homes would not be seen as successful through the discriminating eyes of a world-class chef. Our new workout routine that is effectively getting us in shape might be pathetic to an Olympic athlete. Anything we do might be seen as not enough in someone else's eyes. If we are measuring our success through other people, then our successes can often be distorted into looking more like failures.

Success from God's perspective is something completely different from success in the world's eyes. In order to deal with our fear of failure, we must define true success. Thankfully, the Bible has a lot to say about that!

RELATIONAL OR CIRCUMSTANTIAL?

Close your eyes and think about the ultimate set of circumstances for your life. The ultimate appearance, the ultimate performance, the ultimate car and house and frequent-flyer plan—would those bring you lasting satisfaction? If all these circumstances fell into place, would your soul's thirst be quenched? I think that if you were at all honest with yourself, you would say no. It would be nice, but all of these materialistic perks wouldn't really cut it.

Believe it or not, the Israelites also struggled with material things driving their definition of success. In light of that, God, through their leader Joshua, gave them some advice about where true success lies. The children of Israel, after wandering in the wilderness for forty years, were about to close the ultimate real estate deal and enter the Promised Land. Right before they did, Joshua heard from God and relayed this message to the people: "Do not let this Book of the Law depart from your mouth; meditate on it day and night, so that you may be careful to do everything written in it. Then you will be prosperous and successful" (Joshua 1:8).

Do you see any extraneous circumstances here by which they were to measure success? Do you see anything about the weather, Wall Street, superiority over enemies? Any contingencies? No. This text just says to meditate on the Word of God day and night. Be careful to do everything written in it, and then you will be prosperous and successful. This is a conditional statement—the condition is obedience. You can have all the materialistic trappings of what the world calls success, but without the favor of God, without the pleasure of being in His will, you do not have what the Bible calls success.

We read in Jeremiah 9:23-24 a similar admonition to follow the commands of the Lord in order to know success: "This is what the Lord says: 'Let not the wise boast of their wisdom or the strong boast of their strength or the rich boast of their riches, but let the one who boasts boast about this: that they have the understanding to know me, that I am the Lord, who exercises kindness, justice and righteousness on earth, for in these I delight,' declares the Lord."

Understanding and knowing God: that is a relational thing, not a circumstantial thing. Our culture cries that success is about circumstances, looks, money, power, and prestige. It is not; success is about a personal relationship. It is about knowing God's Word, understanding it, and living it out. It is about having an interactive connection with Him. A lot of us fear this relationship. We say to ourselves, "If I accept Him, I'm going to fail Him. If I try to live a godly life, I know I will fail, and God will judge me, so what is the point of trying?" We have the fear of failure even regarding the one relationship that will give us success.

Guess what? All followers of the Lord fail. We saw earlier how Peter failed the Lord miserably on three separate occasions in one dismal night. Just like Peter, I will fail the Lord and so will you. But that is the beauty of the gospel of Christ: Jesus specializes in taking failures like you and me and reshaping us by His grace. Do you want to find success? Then you must understand, first of all, that success is built on a relationship with God through Christ, not on the circumstances of wealth, position, talent, power, or anything else this world has to offer.

CHARACTER OR ACHIEVEMENT?

When we think of success, we often think of CEOs, corner offices, becoming partner, etc. But all the biblical objectives of success are character driven, not achievement driven. It doesn't matter whether you are a carpenter, commodities broker, coach, teacher, professor, or whatever. God says it doesn't matter: what matters is character. If you have a godly character, if you reflect the nature and character of the Lord in all you do, then you will be successful no matter what your material achievements are. Is that a great deal or what?

First Peter 1:6-7 is one of my favorite passages in the Bible dealing with character development. It focuses first on our failures, then moves to the glory that will be revealed through Christ's success in our lives: "In all this you greatly rejoice, though now for a little while you may have had to suffer grief in all kinds of trials. These have come so that the proven genuineness of your faith—of greater worth than gold, which perishes even though refined by fire—may result in praise, glory and honor when Jesus Christ is revealed." Does God sometimes cause us to fail, falter, and experience trials? Yes. We need trials and failure because God uses trials to discipline us, and discipline leads to growth. God wants us to grow up and make us into better people. He will allow trials and temptations, difficulties, and even failures in order to produce character in our lives. Instead of letting failure define our destiny, God can use failure to fuel our future as we learn to trust Him completely, regardless of the circumstances.

The perennial example of this is Job—not Steve Jobs, but Job of the Old Testament. When I think of the trials and tribulations Job faced, I realize that the hardships in my life are a joke in comparison. God allowed everything to be taken from Job—his possessions, his livelihood, and even his family.

But the one thing that could not be taken away was his faith. The Enemy had the power to affect everything else in Job's life of a materialistic nature, but he could not touch Job's faith.

Because of his faith, Job persevered and his character won that day. God knew the deep commitment of Job and that the testing of his faith would produce an even greater commitment. Job could have failed. He had the freedom of choice to trust God or to curse Him. He chose to trust Him. God knows what we can take, and He tests us accordingly. The apostle Paul tells us that God will not allow us to be tempted beyond what we can bear: "No temptation has seized you except what is common to man. And God is faithful; He will not let you be tempted beyond what you can bear. But when you are tempted, He will also provide a way out, so that you can stand up under it" (1 Corinthians 10:13, BSB). If we fail, it's not because it was more than we could bear. We fail because we are not tapping into the resources God has given us for success: the Holy Spirit of God, the Word of God, and the power of prayer. Each time we stand up under the temptation, the trial, the hardship, the urge to quit, or the desire or to bail out, our character becomes that much stronger for the next time we are tested.

Trials come in different makes and models. We experience small trials and big trials, small failures and big failures. God uses it all, good and bad, to work together for good, "And we know that in all things God works for the good of those who love him, who have been called according to His purpose" (Romans 8:28). What is the key here? This promise is for those who love God. It is for those who are called and who work out

His plans and His purposes in their lives. So often we quote the beginning of this verse and conveniently leave off the last part. God wants good things for us His children. He wants to use everything that happens in our lives, whether good or bad, whether joyful or hurtful, for our own good and for His ultimate glory. But God's provision for us in this area is built upon a relationship of love, of mutual love—His for us and ours for Him. If you belong to God, if you have established that love relationship with Him, He will allow the trials and temptations of life to be of benefit to you. Though you may not always understand how, He is working through all of these things to make us better people of faith.

The last part of 1 Peter 1:7 reads, "These have come so that the proven genuineness of your faith—of greater worth than gold, which perishes even though refined by fire—may result in praise, glory and honor . . ." I think the reason Simon Peter brings up gold here is twofold. I think he is saying that faith is worth more than even the finest material possession, and I think he's using the analogy of a goldsmith to say that God controls the temperature of the trials and failures.

A goldsmith goes through a long process to purify gold. He pours liquid gold into a smelting furnace and cranks up the temperature. As he heats it up, impurities rise to the surface and he scrapes them off until he can see his reflection in it. God has poured you and me into His smelting furnace. He turns up the heat with trials and failures, and all the impurities in our lives rise to surface—anger, bitterness, envy, and pride—where He can scrape them off. When He can see the reflection of

His character in our lives, He knows we're ready to go. What kind of failures are you facing? What is fear doing to you? It's probably a gift from God, to cleanse you of impurities and make you ready for service.

* * *

From the time I was twelve years old to the age of nineteen, it was my goal to play major college basketball. I thought that if those circumstances fell into place, I would have achieved ultimate success.

I was fortunate enough to receive a scholarship to Florida State University, and during my sophomore year, I broke into the starting lineup. I had several key opportunities to shine and do well. I was playing great in practice, but during games, I failed. I could not understand why this was happening. This was my dream. Why would God not allow me to play better in games? Did He not want me to fulfill my dreams?

I believe that God shut the door on that dream in order to find a better dream. I believe that He allowed me to fail because if I had succeeded like I should have, I would be at least four years behind where I am today spiritually, relationally, and emotionally. I would have stayed at Florida State and done the whole college athletics deal. Instead, God tapped me on the shoulder and said, "Ed, I want you to give up your full scholarship and go into ministry." What would people think? What would my family think? I would be lying if I didn't tell you that I was fearing failure on all fronts.

I walked into my coach's office and said, "Coach Williams, I feel led to go into the ministry. I appreciate everything you and the university have done for me, but I want to give up the scholarship." This was very difficult for me because I identified with the game of basketball for so many years. It meant taking a huge risk. It meant giving up what I thought would bring me success and fulfillment and trusting God to give me satisfaction in life.

Yes, in a sense, I had failed at my dream. But through that failure, God taught me something: success is not scoring twenty points a game or being on the all-conference team. I learned through that experience that God uses failure for greater purposes. I also began to understand the nature of true success.

Success from God's perspective is character driven. I learned that, even though I failed at my dream of being a successful college basketball player, I was successful because I was living my life as a Christian witness. I realized that God allowed that failure to happen to get me out of one situation and put me somewhere else. He developed my character through that season and spoke purpose over me, and that is better than any material achievement in my book. At the time, I didn't perfectly understand this, I didn't see the whole picture. But I managed to say, "God, I trust you."

What failure are you going through? What trial are you going through? Are you denying it, dwelling on it, and blaming others for it? Or are you saying, "God, I don't get it now, but I want you to use this time to develop me"? It's all about character. God wants to see courage, commitment, discipline, and vision. He doesn't care how many zeroes appear on the paycheck or how many toys and trinkets we collect. He doesn't care where we live or what we drive. Godly character drives true success.

MANAGEMENT OR OWNERSHIP?

Success in the world is measured by how much we own, how much we accumulate, and how many toys we collect. But in the eyes of God, we don't own one thing. We came into this life with nothing, and we'll leave with nothing.

You may be thinking, "Well, Ed, you don't understand, man. I pulled myself up by my bootstraps. You don't realize what I have made of my life, coming from the background I have." How did you get where you are? Who gave you the creativity, the drive, the people skills to get you there? Who blessed you, enabled you, and empowered you? God gave it to you with the snap of a finger, and He can take it away just as quickly.

Jesus illustrated this idea beautifully with the parable of the talents in Matthew 25. Jesus told His disciples a story about a wealthy landowner who was going out of town on a business trip. Before leaving, he gave one of his servants five talents, another two talents, and a third one talent, with the hopes that they would invest the money for him while he was away. In the time of Jesus, the talent was the largest unit of silver and equivalent to the value of an ox.

During the landowner's absence, here is what happened. The servant with five talents invested in tech stocks, or something like that, and doubled his money. The one with who had two talents parleyed his into four talents. And the one with one talent dug a hole and sat on it.

The wealthy landowner came back in town and checked the accounts. He said to the first two servants, "Good for you. You were faithful with little; now I'll entrust you with a lot." But to the servant who sat on his talent he said, in effect, "Get out of my face," and divided the talent among the others.

What is the point of this story? God rewards productivity! God will even in some cases take from the unproductive and reward the productive. Jesus tells us we should develop our gifts and abilities. I am to invest my gifts, abilities, and talents and use them and invest them as an act of worship to God. I am not supposed to take my abilities and sit on them. I should use them within the context of marriage, within the context of the local church, and within the context of a career for the glory of God to advance His kingdom.

As I develop this gift and give it back to God, God will say, "Well done. I've given you the ability to communicate, to make money, to organize, to be creative. You've developed those abilities, and that's an act of worship." But a lot of us are selfish and greedy. As our earnings go up, our yearnings go up, and we just throw pocket change at God and the church. Our greed and selfishness can easily keep us from God's will. The truth is, we really don't have any stuff. All we have belongs to God. Investing our gifts and abilities is not about giving back to God. We are investing what is already His to begin with.

Success is about managing what our Lord has given us, not owning possessions we think we've earned. And that includes the talents and skills He has given us. We did not earn those or deserve those. God gave us all that we have and all that we are to bring glory to Him, to serve Him, and to minister to others. That is stewardship.

Now that we have a better understanding of biblical success, let's take a look at how some people in the Bible have dealt with the fear of failure.

WHO ARE YOU LISTENING TO?

Perception of other people's opinions of us can really weigh us down. We start thinking we need to look and act like everyone around us and judge others who don't fit the mold. We spend more time developing the person that we think others want us to be rather than embracing our uniqueness and the purpose that God has in store for us. The Israelites were not immune to this way of thinking. They looked around at the surrounding countries and said, "God, the neighboring nations have a king. How come we don't have a king? We want a king!" Parents today may recognize similar tantrums: "Mom, Johnny has that video game, why can't I get it?" or "Dad, they get to stay out until midnight; it's not fair!"

God said, "You don't know what you're asking for, but OK. I'll give you a king." Samuel, God's prophet, tapped Saul on the shoulder for the job. Saul was gifted, articulate, handsome, and tall—head and shoulders above other people. Saul's peers, the guys he had gone to Palestine High with, started making fun of him. They said things like, "What, Saul as a king? What a joke!" (see 1 Samuel 10:11).

Saul tuned into those conversations and thought, "Maybe I am a joke. Maybe I'd be a terrible king." He fell into the trap that many of us fall into by listening to others before listening to God. The approval of his peers meant more to Saul than the calling of God on his life.

Samuel set up a big press conference at Mizpah to announce Saul to the entire nation of Israel. It was time for Saul to go public. But when the big moment arrived, they couldn't find him. He was hiding behind the baggage, consumed with the fear of failure. He had let the opinion of his peers feed his fears, and Saul literally tried to hide from his responsibility before God and the people of Israel.

Do you do that? Are others' words keeping you from a great plan, dream, or aspiration? Are you hiding behind baggage? Has God impressed something on your heart that He wants you to do? Are you being pulled in a certain direction by the gentle leading of the Holy Spirit? But instead of listening to God and drawing strength from Him, are you tuning into the negativity of others?

Think of Noah by way of contrast to Saul. Noah was building a huge boat on dry land at a time when no one had ever seen rain before. People were probably laughing at him, making fun of him. Can you imagine the ridicule he must have faced? But he didn't do what Saul did; he didn't hide behind a stack of lumber or drive the forklift into the back forty. He just kept building. Sure, Noah was fearful; he was human. But he faced his fears. And because he heard the voice of God rather than the negative talk, he went to higher ground while the naysayers and the trash-talkers drowned.

You have a choice to make about whose words and opinions are going to be more important in your estimation. Will you be like Saul? Will you be so fearful of what others think that you literally hide yourself from the responsibilities and opportunities that await you? Or will you be like Noah? Will you listen to God and trust Him to give you strength to persevere even in the midst of negative pressure from others?

WHAT ARE YOU FOCUSED ON?

If we are to understand failure, we also have to come to grips with our strengths and weaknesses. Even Moses, the great patriarch of Jewish faith, the receiver of the law, the deliverer of the children of Israel out of the hands of Pharaoh, had weaknesses. One day, Moses stood trembling in fear before God as a bush burned in front of him, reciting the weaknesses he perceived would keep him from success.

God said, "Moses, I want you to deliver the children of Israel out of Egypt. I want you to talk to them and share my vision with them." Moses said, "No way, God. I stutter and stumble. I can't speak in front of people." Moses was looking at his weaknesses, his shortcomings, and his failures. He was frozen with anxiety and fear.

Is God telling you to do something, only to hear a similar response from you? Are you giving in to your weaknesses and thinking to yourself, "Oh, no, God can't use a failure like me." God heard and understood Moses' fears He knew what Moses' weaknesses were. The issue, though, was not Moses' weakness; it was Moses' lack of trust in God's power.

Think also of David, the shepherd boy turned king. David fought Goliath when he was just a teenager, while he was still going through puberty. While still listening to the popular music, with pimples all over his face, having never fought another human being, he took on Goliath: a nine-foot, 550-pound giant with a major chip on his shoulder. What was David's secret to success? He played to God's strengths, not his own. He said, "I have taken out the lion. I have taken out the bear. I can do it, God is on my side, and he will give me victory." God provided the resources—the stones and the sling—and David, through faith, took the giant out.

Are you giving in to your weaknesses, focusing on them instead of God's power? God can use you in spite of your shortcomings! Consider 2 Corinthians 12:9-10, "But He said to me, 'My grace is sufficient for you, for my power is made perfect in weakness.' Therefore I will boast all the more gladly about my weaknesses, so that Christ's power may rest on me. That is why for Christ's sake, I delight in weaknesses, in insults, in hardships, in persecutions, in difficulties. For when I am weak, then I am strong." Is that your attitude towards weakness? Are you focusing on yourself and your inabilities or on God and His abilities?

One of the greatest paradoxes of the Christian life is that God's power is made known and realized through the weaknesses of His people. If you want to break through to success, you have to focus not on your strength or lack thereof, but on God's strength being made perfect in your shortcomings. Then, and only then, does God truly receive the glory for everything you do because others can clearly see that your accomplishments are made possible by God's powers, not yours.

HOW WILL YOU RESPOND?

The Israelites were standing on the edge of the Promised Land for the first time, and God told them to send out twelve spies to check the land. Ten of the twelve came back and said, "Oh, no, we can't do it! There are giants in the land. The sons of Anak are there." Believe it or not, the sons of Anak were distant relatives of Goliath. "We can't do it. The cities are fortified. The walls are thirty feet thick." They were exaggerating the obstacles to justify their fears and unwillingness to do what needed to be done.

How did the other two spies respond? Basically, they came back and said, "God has promised us this land, and we can overcome." They did not exaggerate the obstacles in their path but rather engaged in the task to which God had called them.

Maybe you'll recognize more readily these modern-day

excuses. "I can't start this business—I don't have the capital, and all of these government requirements are too hard for me to understand." Or how about this: "I'll never be able to make sense of my blended family—the kids fight all the time, and these joint custody arrangements are never going to work out." Or maybe this is more familiar: "If I told the truth to my boss about what happened, I'd be fired. It's not worth the risk to be honest." We still love to exaggerate the obstacles in our lives today. Because we fear an uncertain outcome and don't trust God for success, we exaggerate and rationalize rather than engage. But it is only when we engage that God is able to do more through us than we could imagine.

If you're yielded to His agenda, His timing, and His strength, failure is not an option because God is not a failure. When fear leaves us paralyzed, we need to remember that we are not seeing the whole picture. There is more to come. As long as we keep moving forward, pursuing a relationship with God, developing our character, and stewarding the talents and gifts He's given us, then we are successful—and no one can ever take that away.

CHAPTER 5

SELF-QUARANTINED

FEAR OF LONELINESS

It was the first day of school in the fifth grade and the first time in my life I felt completely alone. My family had just moved from a storybook small town. I abruptly went from a picturesque elementary school to what was basically a maximum-security prison. I had gone from pine trees to the prison yard!

My sentence at this new school began as I walked into a loud and chaotic classroom on the first day. I met my teacher, Mrs. Blackwell, who stood about 5'10" and weighed maybe 100 pounds. She had the worst breath ever! With a deep, raspy voice she said, "Hello, Edwin. Welcome to our school." I was scared and desperately wanted to escape, but my body kept moving forward.

She said, "Here's an empty desk." I sheepishly looked around and put my supplies on the desk. Suddenly, this kid with wild blonde hair and hate in his eyes walked up to me. With the whole class watching, he violently slammed all of my books and supplies against the wall. Stunned, I stepped back, clearly expecting a response from Mrs. Blackwell. Nothing! The only person in the room who had any power to act was silent. That was my first experience with bullying. However, that blonde kid wasn't even the worst bully. He was just an appetizer of sorts for what was to come my way.

I spent most of the morning scanning the crowds for a friendly face. No invitations to sit down at lunch, no understanding nods from a fellow outsider, not one word or smile from anyone.

I felt totally alone. I thought, "I just have to make it to recess. I'm kind of athletic and I can meet some people out there." The bell rang for recess, and full of renewed hope, I made my way outside with the rest of the kids.

I strategically walked around the perimeter of this old dirt playground, just trying to make eye contact with any potentially nice person. I saw some kids playing and stood there looking for any sign of an invitation. All hope was quickly lost when this huge, curly-haired kid with steel blue eyes growled, "What in the blank are you doing? You better get your blankety-blank out of here or I'm going to kick your blank all over the playground!"

I was frozen in my fear and confusion. I started backing up in retreat. I'd never been cussed out before. Admittedly, I've been cussed out many times since, but that was a first for me! I'll never forget it. After he finished throwing that string of words at me, I spent the next thirty minutes shuffling around the edge of the playground looking down at my shoes, kicking sand and thinking, "Why did Mom and Dad move us here? It's the worst place ever." I was completely alone.

It's wild how many people in the world feel alone. Ironically, we are not alone in feeling alone, but when fear comes in and whispers, "You are alone, no one cares, no one has experienced what you've been through," we feel utterly isolated.

In the midst of the pandemic, we were told to self-quarantine. For a lot of people this made their fear of loneliness rise to the surface. God made us to be relational; He put those longings in us. While desiring relationships is good, fear of loneliness can cripple us and cause us to act in unhealthy ways. When our hearts feel broken with longing and fear of loneliness, we must remember that with God, we are never truly alone. He understands us better than we understand ourselves, He loves us more than we love ourselves.

ALONE IN A CROWD

Even in the midst of people, and sometimes especially in a crowd, our loneliness is magnified. When we find ourselves at a crowded restaurant or a crowded church, looking at people connecting and interacting while we are passed by or overlooked, we feel broken, like we're missing something. As we skim through Instagram or Facebook, we may actually feel more lonely, distant, and isolated as we peer into the lives of hundreds or even thousands of "friends." We even have to ask ourselves, "Has social media actually created a world that is more relational?" Sadly, more often than not the answer is no.

"Social" does not necessarily equal relational or meaningful.

Whether in the middle of great hardship or even under normal conditions, many people are dealing with large amounts of loneliness. Even the people who you see connecting at work or church—they feel and fear the loneliness too. You may be one of these people who know how to mask it. You know how to keep it at arm's length. You know how to explain it away, but the reality is you deal with it on a regular basis.

Loneliness can be defined as being without companionship. It is not the same as being alone. Scripture commands us to take time to be alone with our thoughts, alone with our prayers, in solitude and silence. Sometimes, though, we are afraid to be alone because if we are by ourselves, we will have to deal with our loneliness. Alone is a state of being, while loneliness is a state of mind. Loneliness is a mindset that affects our thoughts, emotions, and behavior. If we are to understand and conquer this fear, we need to take a hard look at our attempts to cover up loneliness and examine the precipitating factors that drive this human condition.

First of all, I want to address the things we do to mask loneliness and the things that keep us from honestly confronting it. We live in a time of constant commotion and activity. The noise of our lives serves as a kind of security blanket against the realization of our need for relational connection. The need for social media notifications and new shows to stream has helped to cover over a deeper need, whether felt or unfelt.

Our tethered connection to technology often keeps us from relating to others because we no longer have to relate to other human beings to accomplish the tasks of day-to-day living. Little do we realize, though, as we go about our technology-driven existence that by our behavior we are encouraging the very thing we fear most: a life of isolation that is devoid of human contact.

Technology is not the only culprit. Our attitude towards people often isolates us from them. Whether because of political differences, divergent lifestyles, or generational divides, we are polarized and often prize our pride and egos over genuine connection. We no longer understand what it means to live in true intimacy and community with others. In short, we are a lonely people, and we have no one to blame but ourselves.

From the very beginning in the Garden of Eden, the Bible tells to us over and over again that it is not good for us to be alone. It would be easy to say, "God does not want you to be alone, so stop fearing loneliness." You can close the book, "The End." But we cannot do that. It is not that simple. The Bible not only cautions us against isolation, but it also shows us how to break down the walls and masks that isolate us. It teaches us how to break through to connectedness on several different levels.

In this chapter, I want to identify three levels of loneliness and then show you how to connect relationally in the midst of them. You may be saying to yourself, "Me, lonely? Are you kidding?" I will guarantee you something. Everyone, including me, deals with one or more of these levels of longing that can lead to loneliness.

Understanding and overcoming the fear of loneliness is critical to living the abundant Christian life. Larry Crabb says it well in his insightful book *Understanding Who You Are:* "Life in Christ is all about relationships, with God, with others, and ourselves. When we reduce Christianity to a series of steps for handling life better or a set of truths to believe or a list of things to do, we miss the whole point of the gospel." In short, it's all about relationships. Loneliness is the symptom of some unmet relational need. Before we dive in, we must first understand that we will never find ultimate relational fulfillment in any relationship until the relational need with God is met.

SPIRITUAL LONGING

God created us so that He could have fellowship with us. The Bible was written that we might know God. Christ came into the world so we could be reconciled to God. Sadly, many people live their lives outside of a relationship with God, and they are spiritually lonely. This represents the first and most significant level of loneliness: *spiritual loneliness.*

The Bible says we are all born lonely, separated from God. The prophet Isaiah put it this way: "But your iniquities have separated you from your God; your sins have hidden his face from you, so that He will not hear" (Isaiah 59:2). When God saw our situation, when He saw the implications of our state of spiritual loneliness, He didn't just say, "Well, too bad for you. I guess you will have to live a spiritually lonely life." God did something: He took the initiative to break the cycle of loneliness.

You may have a gnawing sense that something is not right in your life. You have been on a search for significance. You fear this loneliness that you feel inside of you. You thought that joining a certain club or playing on the right team or climbing the corporate ladder would do it, but nothing has brought the meaning for which you've been searching. You thought making a certain amount of money would do it, but the money has lost its luster. You thought that getting married to that certain person would do it, but that, too, has left you empty. You thought that having a couple of children to carry on your legacy would do it, but they have not filled the hole in your heart.

You know deep down that you are still lonely. You are spiritually lonely. I don't care what you do or how much money you can pile up, how many toys and things you can accumulate. Those things will not fill that void in your life. Maybe you need to deal with this first level of loneliness in the most basic and fundamental sense. Maybe you need to allow Jesus Christ to come into your life so you can be reconciled with God.

We serve an initiative-taking God. When God saw our loneliness, this chasm, a gap caused by our sinfulness, He sent Jesus to live a perfect life and to die on the cross for our sins and rise again. That is the message of Christianity. When Jesus was dying on the cross, what did He say? Some of His last words were chilling: "My God, my God, why have you forsaken me?" (Matthew 27:46). Why have you, God, turned your back on me? Why this loneliness, God? When Jesus was hanging on the cross, God the Father had to turn His back on His Son. He had to separate Himself from His Son. As He paid for our sins, Jesus felt this spiritual level of loneliness to the point we cannot even express in words. He did not want us to go through an eternity missing true community with God. He paved the way for us to have a personal relationship with God the Father.

It is our loneliness that drives us to our knees. It is our loneliness that motivates us to become Christ followers. Talk to people who have been followers of the Lord for years and years. They will tell you that they felt lonely—a gnawing sense that something was wrong. They had holes in their hearts that brought them to a place of receiving Christ. Maybe you are there with that same gnawing feeling at the core of your being. You can satisfy your spiritual longings only by establishing a personal relationship God, and it all begins by placing your faith and trust in Jesus Christ.

What if you're a believer? What if you are like me and you know Christ personally, but now and then you still feel a sense of loneliness? We know if you have accepted Christ, then you can never experience true loneliness again. But we can still have feelings of loneliness from time to time. What do we do with those feelings when loneliness rears its ugly head and tries to knock us down? We can either take those feelings of loneliness and let them push us away from God, or we can allow those feelings to push us toward God. We can pray, "God, I'm having feelings of loneliness. I know I am not truly alone because I know you. But I'm still feeling the feelings.

God, fill the gap in my life. Help me, God, with Your grace, love, and power, to experience You in a deeper way to satisfy these spiritual longings in my heart."

The apostle Paul experienced loneliness. In 2 Timothy 4:16, he declared, "At my first defense, no one came to my support, but everyone deserted me." Have you ever felt that you are the only person standing for Christ at the office? Do you feel like you are the only real Christian around the neighborhood? Or perhaps you may even be standing alone for Christ in your family. You are the only one in your family who made a faith commitment, and sometimes the feelings of loneliness are unbearable. Paul continues in verse 17, "But the Lord stood at my side and gave me strength." We must recognize our need for and draw strength from the companionship of Christ.

What did Jesus say to His disciples right before He left the earth and went to heaven? "And surely I am with you always, to the very end of the age" (Matthew 28:20). Do you have that spiritual loneliness quenched? Have you met God through Christ? Or if you know Him, are you allowing the feelings of loneliness that sometimes assault you to push you closer and deeper in your relationship with Him? Christ has always been there; He is waiting for you to make a move toward Him.

RELATIONAL LONGING

I call the next level of loneliness relational loneliness. If you go back to the first book of the Bible, Genesis, and read over the first two or three chapters, you will see God creating. After every creative act, God stepped back and said, "It is good." Then God made man in His image and said, "It is very good." Adam, the first man, was fulfilled in his spiritual connectedness; he was connected with God. He was interacting with Him in a way that we will not experience until we get to heaven.

Something suddenly changes in Genesis 2:18. God saw a problem and He labeled something as "not good" for the first time, "The Lord God said, 'It is not good for the man to be alone. I will make him a helper suitable for him'" (Genesis 2:18).

God did not deny that Adam had a need for human companionship. God did not try to explain it away. He said there was a need and that He would make someone suitable for Adam. God took the initiative with Adam and He took the initiative again with Christ. We serve a God who steps out of the shadows and is proactive. God's game plan is basic. He wants us to have a vibrant connection through Christ. He wants us to walk deeply in our relationships with others. That is God's agenda for our lives.

Jesus summarized the importance of these two longings, spiritual and relational, in a couple of succinct sentences in Matthew 22:37-39. In response to a question about which was the greatest commandment, He said, "'Love the Lord your God (*this indicates intention*) with all your heart and with all your soul and with all your mind (*this indicates the level of intensity*).' This is the first and greatest commandment. And the second is like it: 'Love (*intention*) your neighbor as yourself (*intensity*)'" (parenthetical comments added).

So we have intentionality, a decision to love, followed by intensity. An intentional decision to love God with all of your being comes first. And an intentional decision to love others as yourself comes second.

The Bible never tells us to love ourselves. That is a given. I love myself. You love yourself too. But when I am asked to love my neighbor as myself, that is a tall order. You might say, "I want to have deep relationships. I really want to connect with others." Many of us say that, but in reality, we don't mean it. The truth of the matter is that most people, including Christians, have surface-level relationships. We may have known people for a long time, but we are still talking about the same stuff: the weather, sports, and current events. We are fearful to relate to them on a deep level. Why? We say to ourselves, "If they knew all of my problems, they would reject me. They wouldn't like me. They would not believe what I am dealing with or what I have done or what I am struggling with. They would just keep me at arm's length." In an effort to not feel the loneliness of rejection, we isolate ourselves and feel the loneliness of not being truly known. If we were to come clean about our spiritual and relational loneliness and really begin to share who we are with people, they would probably sigh and tell us they are struggling with the same issues.

The key is to keep both of these levels of loneliness in balance. Do not expect other people to fix your spiritual loneliness or expect God to fill the relational void in your life. You were created for relationship with God and community— not one or the other. You cannot expect your spouse to meet needs that only God can meet. You can't put those types of expectations on your wife or your husband or your friend. My friends can't deliver me from evil. My friends cannot answer my prayers. My friends cannot forgive me of my sins or guide me or lead me. Only God can do that. If we turn to human relationships to satisfy our relational loneliness before turning to God to satisfy our spiritual loneliness, we are in for trouble. We cannot dump all of our longings and feelings of loneliness on human relationships. We must first bring our loneliness to God, and then we will be able to feel more satisfied and fulfilled in our relationships.

Sometimes we rely so much on other people to take away our feelings of loneliness that we become clingy. We put so much pressure on the other person that we totally turn them off to wanting to relate to us at all. They begin to say, "Man, I need some space. You are smothering me." They push us away, and we feel rejected. If or when this happens, go back to God and recognize the spiritual longing you have neglected. Your Savior must be the source of your relational strength. When you connect with Him, when you walk with Him, when you talk with Him, then you have some real power to bring to human relationships. A true friend is going to point you to Christ. A true friend will deepen your relationship with Him. Do you really want those deep-water relationships? Let me give several suggestions to help make this happen on a practical level.

First, take regular relational risks. Every time we take a relational risk, we are reflecting the character and nature of

God. When we do not take those risks, when we hide behind our fears, we are disobeying God. Now when I say relational risk, it might not be the kind of risk you are thinking of. It's not about adventurous and dangerous "James Bond" kind of stuff. No, what I mean by relational risk is the boldness of being friendly. Although it might not seem like it on the surface, if you really think about it, friendliness is a very vulnerable and bold action. Proverbs 18:24 says, "A man who has friends must himself be friendly" (NKJV). We all want friends. And if you want to have friends, you need to ask yourself a couple of questions. What kind of friend would I like to have? Am I willing to be that kind of friend?

I have moved around many times in my life. I have moved from Canton, North Carolina; to Taylors, South Carolina; to Columbia, South Carolina; to Houston, Texas; to Tallahassee, Florida; back to Houston, Texas; and from there to Dallas, Texas. A while back, I was thinking about the deep relationships God has given me over the years even though I moved around a lot. I asked myself what the common thread was in those relationships. What quality or qualities made those relationships work? Then it came to me. I have taken the initiative in almost every relationship I have had. I have taken regular relational risks. I knew that if I was going to have deep friendships, I had to show myself friendly. More than that, I had to be vulnerable with those whom I wanted to develop deeper relationships.

Here is what many of us do in the church in regard to relationships. Week in and week out, we walk into the church, and we look for a seat. We think to ourselves, "Boy, there sure are a lot of people here. This is a big church." We find our seat and we just sit there. And then after a while, maybe several months, we say to ourselves, "No one talked to me. No one came up to me. This church is just not a friendly place. It is full of snobs." Then we go to another church and do the same thing again. After a while we say, "No one talked to me. No one came up to me. I guess this church is just full of snobs too. No one cares about me. I want to relate to people. I want to talk to people, but no one comes up to me."

God does not want to hear those weak excuses. He wants you to take relational risks. A person who wants a friend must show himself to be a friendly person. It's time to step out and see what God has in store for you.

The church is to be a social place. I am not just making this up. Read about the early church in Acts 2. They met together in the temple courts, and they met from house to house. They didn't just silently show up to a Sunday service and leave as soon as the pastor said "Amen" in the closing prayer. They were highly social and highly relational in every aspect of what they did as a church body. If we are going to reach the level of the community exhibited by the early church, we must take the relational risks necessary to bring people into the inner spheres of our lives.

The Bible tells us that we are to show hospitality to others, especially to our brothers and sisters in the Lord: "Offer hospitality to one another without grumbling" (1 Peter 4:9). I am talking about that initiative-taking, house-warming, guest-comforting mentality that says, "Come out with us for a hamburger," or "Come over and let's enjoy a meal together." That is hospitality. Is your life marked with a spirit of hospitality?

The Lord hit me with a bolo punch a few years ago regarding what hospitality really is. I was on a mission trip in Korea with Lisa. A missionary invited us over to her two-room house to spend the night. She served us Spam on crackers with Kool-Aid. She threw a mat on the floor for us to sleep on. This generous woman was hospitable with what God had given her. Hospitality is sharing what you have with others for the glory of God. Yet a lot of us here in America live in three-, four-, five-, or six-bedroom homes and have not invited anyone over yet. We throw out these lame excuses for not opening up our homes: "It would take me too long to clean the house and get it ready," "I want to furnish and decorate the house just right before I have people over to see it," "I can't really cook that well," "I don't know what to say to my guests."

The purpose of hospitality is not to impress our friends or to raise our social status up a notch. Hospitality is about community, about providing an outlet where real relationships can grow. It is about honoring your guests and valuing them as people. It is about taking away someone's feelings of loneliness and meeting a relational need they have. It's about an open invitation to open up. You will find that if you just make some small attempts at hospitality, you will enjoy it and wish you had started doing it much earlier.

You may remember the story of Jesus going to the home

of Martha and her sister Mary for a meal. Martha was busying herself with all the cooking, the preparations, the cleaning, and so on. She wanted to impress her Lord. She wanted to be noticed for all she was doing and she complained to Jesus that Mary was not doing any of the work but was getting all the attention.

Mary was sitting at the feet of Jesus talking and listening to Him. She wanted to know Jesus. She did not want to be noticed as much as she wanted to notice, observe, and learn from all Jesus had to offer. Her purpose was to get to know Him and value Him as her guest.

For Mary and Jesus, a simple meal and good conversation were all that was required. But Martha went overboard. In all her busyness, she forgot why Jesus was there in the first place. I love Jesus' reply to Martha in response to her complaint because it cuts to the core of Martha's problem: "My dear Martha, you are worried and upset over all these details! There is only one thing worth being concerned about. Mary has discovered it, and it will not be taken away from her" (Luke 10:41-42, NLT).

Remember the why of hospitality. Do not be worried and upset about all the things you think you need to do to entertain your guests. The Lord of lords required only a simple meal and fellowship with His hosts. The same simplicity is all He asks of you as you open up your home to others.

The writer of Hebrews said, "Do not forget to entertain strangers, for by so doing some people have entertained angels without knowing it" (Hebrews 13:2). I can't promise anything, but by practicing hospitality to friends and strangers alike, you never know whom God might send your way.

Taking it a step deeper, the entire church should be built on hospitality. This is best done through small groups. Yes, we are commanded to worship God corporately, but we also must connect in small-group settings. One of the things we say often at Fellowship Church is that we want to grow smaller while we grow larger.

Again, don't let fear dictate your actions in this regard. It is easy to make excuses for not getting involved in a small group. "Well, Ed, they might ask me a question about the Bible, and I don't know that much about the Bible. They might put me on the spot." I am not talking about attending a seminary class. A small group is a place where you can learn about God's Word together and find ways to apply it to your lives together. You are not going to be tested or prodded or poked. At least, if it is a biblically functioning group within a biblically functioning church, you should not be. We have to connect in this way in order to build community. We have to connect intimately with people in order to deal with the loneliness we all feel. We have to connect because of the value each of us brings to the small-group table. We cannot let circumstance keep us from connecting or hinder our heart for helping connect others.

What are the benefits of going deeper relationally? Let me hit a couple of them briefly. First of all, it will mature you like nothing else will. When you think about spiritual maturity, when you study it in the Bible, it is always centered on *others*. We are to love one another, serve one another, help one another, encourage one another, comfort one another—I could go on and on. It is about getting outside of yourself and deepening your faith by articulating it to others and welcoming others in the name of the Lord.

Going deeper relationally will also broaden your horizons. Not everyone grew up the way you did or had the same kind of parents you did. Not everyone went to the same college you did or had the same hardships you did. You will get to know people who have different perspectives on life—those who can share with you some valuable lessons from their unique experiences. There are people all around you in your church, neighborhood, and office who have something to offer to you relationally, if you will only reach out and take the risk. Make a move to deepen your relationships and share your resources. When we do this, we begin to understand on a very practical level that is what God did for us.

ETERNAL LONGING

There is a third level of loneliness that is related to our spiritual loneliness, but it is really a longing unto itself. It is a loneliness that longs for eternity in heaven. It is that eternal quenching that will occur when we move from this life into an eternal rest in heaven. This eternal quenching is really the culmination of all of our longings because it will ultimately satisfy our spiritual and relational longings forever. Revelation 21:4 speaks of heaven, saying that God "'will wipe every tear . . . There will be no more death' or mourning or crying or pain, for the old order of things has passed away." We are wired up for a happy ending. Everything in our lives points toward it, and it will only be fully realized in heaven.

Ecclesiastes 3:11 says, "He has also set eternity in the hearts of men" (BSB). Because God has placed these eternal longings in our hearts, true fulfillment will occur only in eternity. This is the final hope of the people who have placed their trust in Christ. When we are finally home, we will never be lonely again.

* * *

Fear of loneliness can sap us of strength and leave us unfulfilled. We fear loneliness and yet we also fear rejection which can lead us to only pursuing half-hearted relationships. Don't be afraid to be fully known, by God and by others. Only then will you be able to vaccinate yourself from the fear of loneliness. If you are fully known, then you are never alone.

When God is with you, you are never alone. But when those feelings of loneliness crop up, they can discourage you and make you feel alone. In these moments, I encourage you to press in. Get on your knees and tell God exactly how you are feeling. He is the ultimate comforter, and as we seek Him regularly, He will dissolve any fear of loneliness with His perfect love.

CHAPTER 6

100 PERCENT

FEAR OF DEATH

I've always been fascinated by sharks. For as long as I can remember, I've read about them, drawn them, and watched them. But nothing compares to swimming with them. I was once in the Bahamas with Stuart Cove, the number one shark diver in the world. I, on the other hand, was a beginner with a capital B. So, I found it a little unsettling when Stuart said, "The most important thing to know about sharks is: if they want you, they're going to have you."

I asked Stuart if he had any fear of sharks, and he said, "Well, today, we'll be baiting the sharks and creating a situation. I don't have 'fear' but more of a respect for them." I liked that. Respect the shark.

As we prepared to get in the water, I was both nervous and excited. The boat arrived at its destination and sharks were everywhere. There were about forty of these monsters around the boat—some up to nine feet long. I asked Stuart, "I just dive in on top of them? It doesn't matter?" He said, "They'll move. Just keep your hands in. We'll be feeding them with pieces of fish that look like the palm of your hand." I repeated to myself, "Keep your hands in." Stuart added, "They'll be bumping into us, so don't pull on their tails." Got it. No tails.

I was standing on the back of the boat with my toes on the edge. I could feel my heart pounding. No turning back now. "Just lean back, Ed" I said to myself. My adrenaline was pumping as I fell into the water full of dozens of frenzied sharks. It was a thrilling experience, but also frightening. I had confidence in these very experienced shark divers who were with me. I also had confidence that the growing cloud of sharks swarming around me could end my life very quickly.

However, once I was down there a few minutes and saw how beautiful, magical, and peaceful it was, I was fine. I was thankful to have the experience. But I never forgot the fear. I'm glad I faced the fear of death.

The fear of death is pretty universal. We all know that one day we will die, and that thought terrifies many of us. For example, in the midst of a pandemic, we hear statistics and updates from the news and media about the number of deaths around the world. It is scary, and the fear of death is on everyone's mind. How do we deal with this fear as Christians? On one hand, I know that God controls my life and death. Only He knows my last day on planet Earth. But I also believe we should be wise and take precautions when necessary. We should always practice eating right, exercising, and getting the right amount of sleep. We do so to honor and take care of the body God has entrusted to each one of us. But whether these choices prolong our lives in any way is in God's hands.

Whenever I deliver a sermon about death, I can sense people shifting nervously in their seats. People generally don't like discussions about death. Most people don't want to be reminded that their lives are slipping away. We try to ignore death or mask over it by calling it anything but "death." When someone dies, we say things like: "Their candle has gone out." "He's no longer with us." "She's moved on." "He's gone to be with the Lord." "She passed away, God rest her soul." No matter how we choose to say it, we must face the inevitability of death if we are to conquer the fear of death and live life to the fullest.

I am not going to spend a lot of time trying to convince you about whether or not we die. That is a forgone conclusion. George Bernard Shaw wrote, "The stats on death are quite impressive; one out of one die." There is a 100 percent chance you will die. Have you noticed how much of our news centers on death and dying? Most of what we see on the news is about death. A friend of mine who attends Fellowship Church is an anchorman for a local station. He once told me, "Ed, if it bleeds, it leads." We see examples of this all the time. Whether facing a natural disaster, a tragic accident, or a viral outbreak, the media's coverage gives minute-by-minute updates of the death toll. The data is continually feeding our insecurities and raising our fear quotient.

I think that when we let fear of death cripple us, we aren't able to live life to the fullest as God intends us to. I am not saying that we should all be more reckless, but I think the fear virus can keep us from taking opportunities that God has in store for us. When we reflect on the life that Jesus gave us through dying on the cross and really understand what comes after death, then we are better able to face our fear of death because we have an eternal hope.

WHAT HAPPENS NEXT?

Here is why it matters that we talk frankly about our fear of death: we are going to die, plain and simple. We all know it on some level. But situations like a global pandemic pull back the curtain on just how afraid we actually are of facing death in any form. In this kind of environment, I think it's even more important to speak frankly about death and to reflect on what the hope of Christ's death and resurrection offers us. Let me elaborate some on what happens the moment after we breathe our last breath here and take in our first breath in the hereafter. What's the eternal agenda for your life and mine?

The first item on the agenda, immediately after our bodies die, is that our souls will be transported to an eternal existence in the spiritual realm. What that means for the Christian, a believer in Christ, is an instantaneous trip into the presence of the Lord. For the unbeliever, who will also live on after physical death, the opposite will be true. When they are absent from the body, they will be separated from God in eternity as they await final judgment (which we will address in the next section). When our candle goes out in this life, it will be ignited in the next life. We will immediately exist as our true selves.

Those who hold on to the extinction theory believe, "Once I

die, that's it. It's over for me." Poof, into the void. That is not what God tells us will happen. He says that each of us will move from this life into the next at the moment of physical death. There is life after the grave; we must prepare for that certainty.

Maybe you're saying, "Well, Ed, how do you really know there is life after the grave?" If you don't want to take God's word for it, then look at the cycles of death giving way to life in nature. Take a seed, for instance. The seed looks like it is dead. It seems like it's curtains for the seed, but if you plant the seed, it germinates, and a plant bursts forth. Think about a caterpillar crawling around, an ugly little creature. One day it surrounds itself in a cocoon, which in reality is a tomb, and you think life is history for the ugly insect. Yet soon after, a butterfly bursts forth with brilliant color. Notice the cycles of nature—death giving way to life.

The great physicist Albert Einstein discovered that matter may change states, but it will not be destroyed. Many people who have studied the first law of thermodynamics feel it is a clue to life after the grave. We will change states, but we will not be destroyed. Philosophers also find a rationale for life after death in logic and in the nature of life and existence. Philosophers have studied human beings and observed that all of us have a code of ethics, a sense of justice and fairness. Immanuel Kant said this, "Since justice is not applied fully, it must be applied in the afterlife by a judge who settles all accounts." The Bible says that God is that judge who will deliver ultimate justice in eternity.

Anthropologists will tell you that almost every culture,

d people group they have studied has an advanced view of the afterlife. Yet the Bible speaks with more authority and more urgency than any other book about eternal matters. If you take the words of Jesus regarding eternity and put them up against those of other world religious leaders or gurus, you will see that His words resonate with the conviction of truth.

Also, consider the eight million near-death experiences that have been reported. These people experience physical death for a few seconds or a few minutes, and when they come back, they have a completely new and different perspective on life. My grandfather had a near-death experience right after he became a Christian. It changed his life; he was never the same. You may not put much stock in these types of experiences, but if you spend any amount of time around someone who's gone through one, you might just change your mind.

All of these things point to the reality that the soul lives on immediately after death. The Bible also tells us that at some point in the future, when Christ returns for the second time, both believers and unbelievers will be resurrected. This simply means that the bodies of those who have died will be reunited with their souls. Acts 24:15 tells us plainly, "There will be a resurrection of both the righteous and the wicked." The resurrection of the believer will happen first, prior to Christ setting up His millennial kingdom on the earth. The resurrected believer will have a new glorified body and will reign with Christ on earth for one thousand years in a kingdom of peace, prosperity, and joy. During this time, Satan is bound and unable to wreak havoc on the earth.

The unbeliever who has died, on the other hand, will be resurrected after the millennial kingdom on earth is over. Whereas the body of the believer is raised to honor, the body of the unbeliever, because they rejected the gospel of Jesus Christ, is raised to dishonor.

It is because of the resurrection of Jesus Christ from the dead and our vicarious participation with Him as believers that our bodies will be restored to a glorified and eternal state. What happens after the resurrection, for both the righteous and the wicked, is the next item on our agenda.

THE JUDGMENT

After the resurrection of the dead, the believer and the unbeliever alike will be judged.

What is the purpose of this postmortem meeting? We have a standing appointment to stand before the throne of God. Hebrews 9:27 declares, "Just as people are destined to die once, and after that to face judgment . . ." We live once, die once, and then after that comes the judgment of God. There is no reincarnation. There is no perpetual cycle of birth, death, and rebirth culminating in some unknown day in the ethereal state of nirvana or paradise. The Bible is very specific about the finality of physical death and the reality after that of judgement before the living God.

Whether you are a good guy or a good girl, whether you have paid your taxes, kept your nose clean, or given to charities—

these will not even be brought to the table. These items can't be entered into the agenda. You may say, "I'm Catholic," "I was confirmed," "I was baptized in a Baptist Church," "I am in a small group," "I am an usher at my church," or "My grandfather is Billy Graham." That's great. Good for you. But none of these things will be a deciding factor in this cosmic meeting with God. None of us will be exempt. This, actually, is something all of us should approach with a healthy fear.

Have you ever been unprepared for a business meeting? Have you ever been on your heels with your head spinning, grasping for straws? That's the way it will be for a lot of people, because most people are duped into thinking God grades on the performance plan or on some national average or a cosmic curve. Not so. God's standard is simply His holiness. His standard of perfection is His very own character. All of us are sin-stained in comparison to the holiness of God. I am and you are. If we try to face God on our own pitiful merits, we are in severe trouble.

God will be looking for one thing and one thing only in this meeting. He will look at our lives to see if a cosmic transaction has taken place, if we have received what His Son did for us on the cross. That is the final standard by which we will be judged.

We looked at Hebrews 9:27 earlier: "Just as people are destined to die once, and after that to face judgment"—but the thought continues in verse 28: "so Christ was sacrificed once to take away the sins of many; and He will appear a second time, not to bear sin, but to bring salvation to those who are waiting for Him." Christ came to die once for our sins. We will die once and then, after that, be judged in eternity. When Christ comes again, those who have accepted His forgiveness and committed their lives to Him will be spared God's wrath. Those who have not will condemn themselves by their unbelief.

John 3:16 is perhaps the best-known verse in the Bible. But all too often, we stop after verse 16 and ignore the rest of the passage in verses 17-18: "For God did not send His Son into the world to condemn the world, but to save the world through Him. Whoever believes in Him is not condemned, but whoever does not believe stands condemned already because they have not believed in the name of God's one and only Son." God will not condemn anyone to hell on the day of judgment. Those who have rejected His Son and the salvation from sin offered to all who believe will already stand condemned on that day. They will have already secured on their own a one-way ticket to an eternity separated from the love of God.

As long as we have breath, it is not too late to appropriate what Christ has done for us on the cross. The Bible says we become a Christian by grace through faith. Receiving eternal life is nothing we deserve, nothing we merit. It is a gift given simply by God's unfathomable love.

Ephesians 1:13-14 explains the process by which someone makes this transaction and what occurs: "And you also were included in Christ when you heard the message of truth, the gospel of your salvation. When you believed, you were marked in Him with a seal, the promised Holy Spirit, who is a deposit guaranteeing our inheritance until the redemption of those who are God's possession—to the praise of His glory." God's truth is the same today as it was two thousand years ago when Ephesians was written. You have heard the truth of the gospel. Only you can personally appropriate the gospel for yourself. No one else can do it for you. It is my prayer that many who pick up this book will understand the personal nature of the gospel and that they will accept the gift of eternal life that Christ offers.

The passage goes on to talk about "the promised Holy Spirit" as a seal of our inheritance. I love that word *seal* because when we make the defining-moment decision to receive Christ, our very lives are stamped with the person of God in the form of the Holy Spirit. The seal is binding and irrevocable. This means the transaction is complete and guaranteed until Christ comes back to claim us as His own. If you have been sealed with the Holy Spirit, there is no need to fear your final hour. Death is just a doorway to your final redemption when God claims you as a co-heir with Christ. What does it mean that the Holy Spirit has been given to us as a deposit? The Holy Spirit is still a mystery to many Christians. In our ignorance, we tend to discount the importance of this third person of the godhead. 2 Corinthians 1:21-22 says, "Now it is God who makes both us and you stand firm in Christ. He anointed us, set His seal of ownership on us, and put His Spirit in our hearts as a deposit, guaranteeing what is to come." We receive Christ and the seal is placed on our lives. The transaction has been completed and God has taken title of our lives. On top of that, the Holy Spirit, the person whom Christ places in our lives the moment we receive Him, is our deposit.

Here is what happens when we make the commitment to Christ. Just as fear binds us up, forgiveness frees us up! All of our sinfulness, guilt, shame, and pain are transferred to His shoulders. All of His forgiveness, love, righteousness, and grace are transferred to our shoulders. That is the cosmic transaction. Doesn't that sound like something worth committing to? If you have placed your trust in Christ, you are sealed and the transaction is complete for all eternity. God has purchased you by the precious blood of His Son. You are God's forever. You have nothing to fear; your salvation is secure in the love of Christ.

Again, this meeting with God in eternity will be about only one thing. Has the cosmic transaction been completed in your life or not? At this point you can't take a mulligan. There will be no do-overs. You can't hire a team of attorneys to defend your case before a judge. This meeting is not about anything you have done. It is about something you need to receive: "Yet to all who receive Him, to those who believed in His name, He gave the right to become children of God" (John 1:12).

THE SEPARATION

Let's look at the next item on our agenda: the separation. The Bible describes how Jesus will separate us all into two camps. "All the nations will be gathered before Him, and He will separate the people one from another as a shepherd separates the sheep from the goats" (Matthew 25:32). We either face eternal bliss in heaven or eternal punishment in hell.

It is impossible for us to fathom what heaven will be like. As an inadequate comparison, take the closest you've ever felt to God in this life. It could have been in a church service. It might have been in a small group meeting or at a summer camp. Perhaps it was while listening to a beautiful piece of music. It could have been while you were walking on the beach or in the woods. Even if you were to take that experience and multiply it many times over, it would still fall short of the glory and the connection we will have with God in heaven. You could take the best you've ever felt relationally or the closest you have ever felt with another human being. Multiply that feeling exponentially and it will still fall miserably short of what heaven will be like. You could think about your skills, about a time you were really on a roll using your abilities. It will fall miserably short of how you are going to use your skills in heaven.

The Bible says heaven is also going to be a place where those who have been separated unto Christ will also have a special bodily transformation. I know many people are looking forward to that. I have already mentioned that both the righteous and the wicked will be resurrected, but the Bible promises that the body of a believer will be raised in glory. Paul, in 1 Corinthians 15:42-44, describes this new body as an entirely different kind than our earthly body: "The body that is sown is perishable, it is raised imperishable; it is sown in dishonor, it is raised in glory; it is sown in weakness, it is raised in power; it is sown a natural body, it is raised a spiritual body." This passage goes on to say that our glorified body will be like Christ's: "And just as we have borne the image of the earthly man, so shall we bear the image of the heavenly man" (1 Corinthians 15:49). Those who have been crucified with Christ by receiving Him into their lives will also be raised with Him in glory.

There will be angels in heaven, but we cannot begin to imagine what kind of awesome creatures they are. As for descriptions of their Creator, our words and imaginations fail us. The apostle John had an awesome vision of heaven and of worship around the throne of God. He recorded these words in Revelation 4:6-10:

In the center, around the throne, were four
living creatures, and they were covered
with eyes, in front and in back.
The first living creature was like a lion, the
second was like an ox, the third had a face
like a man, the fourth was like a
flying eagle. Each of the four living
creatures had six wings and was covered
with eyes all around, even under its wings.
Day and night they never stop saying:
"Holy, holy, holy is the Lord God Almighty,
who was, and is, and is to come."
Whenever the living creatures give glory,

honor and thanks to Him who sits on the
throne and who lives forever and
ever, the twenty-four elders fall down
before Him who sits on the throne and
worship Him who lives for ever and ever.

The central focus of heaven will be the eternal praise and worship of God. It will be a place of unencumbered worship and unfettered relationships. There will be no racism, no backbiting, no wars, no division, no tears, and no heartache.

Those who have not claimed Jesus as their Savior in this life will be separated from Him forever in the afterlife. Those who have not been set apart by the Lamb of God for heaven will go to a place called hell. The Bible uses several phrases to describe this place. The first phrase used is *outer darkness* (see Matthew 8:12; 22:13; 25:30, NASB). I talk to people who say, "I don't know if I want to go to heaven with all those goody-goody Christians. I want to go to hell so I can 'raise hell' with my friends. We can party in hell." Even if your friends are in hell, you will not know it. It will be like an eternal solitary confinement. Those who are separated into this camp because of their unbelief will be cast into outer darkness or complete isolation. Hell is likely to be a place where all of your sinful desires can come true, but utterly and completely alone.

In his book *The Great Divorce,* C.S. Lewis wrote a stunning illustration of what hell represents for the person who has lived only for himself in this life and has rejected God. The premise of this fictional book is that, even if given the chance, the unbelieving person in hell would not want to live in heaven. On an imaginary bus ride from the depths of hell to the pinnacle of heaven, Lewis shows the great spiritual divide, the great divorce, that exists between the desires of the believer and those of the unbeliever, between the false comforts of hell and the real rewards of heaven.

In his introduction, Lewis wrote that the book was not to be seen as his personal or theological views on what heaven or hell will actually be like. The purpose of Lewis' story was to present a moral story, a parable, to illustrate that the unbeliever who did not worship God in this life would not be able or willing to do it in the next.

The purpose of Lewis' story was to show that how we spend this life prepares us for eternity. Those of us who worship God in spirit and truth and have faith in Christ will be prepared for the reality of heaven and an eternity spent in the presence of God. Those who worship themselves and live their lives for anything or anyone other than God will be prepared only for an eternity separate from God—in isolation, remorse, and regret.

Here is a description in the book of the mindset of those who live in hell and their continuing desire to be a world unto themselves:

> *They've been moving on and on. Getting*
> *farther apart. They're so far off by now*
> *that they could never think of coming to*
> *the bus stop at all. Astronomical distances.*
> *There's a bit of rising ground near where I*

live and a chap has a telescope. You can see
the lights of the inhabited houses, where
those old ones live, millions of miles away.
Millions of miles from us and from one
another. Every now and then they move
further still.

Millions of miles away. The insurmountable distance represents the spiritual state of those who have lived this life only for themselves and will continue to isolate themselves in eternity. They will be separate from God, separate from His love, and separate from the love and companionship of anyone else, moving further and further into isolation throughout eternity. What a terrible picture of the unregenerate soul. If I were to fear one thing, it would be a fear of isolation from God.

Another phrase the Bible uses about hell is "where the worm never dies and the fire never goes out" (Mark 9:48, NLT). Fourth-century theologian Jerome called hell "a place of sensory torment." It is the forever-painful feeling of isolation and separation from God. "But Ed, how could this good God send good people to hell?" You might ask. "How can God send this nice family member in my life to eternal damnation? I just don't get it. The God I worship would never do such a thing." God does not send anybody to hell. We make that choice ourselves. I mentioned this idea earlier. We are made in the image of God, and thus we have been given the freedom to decide our own fate.

Here is what God will do at the end of our existence. He

will simply give us a greater measure of what we desired on this planet. If we bowed the knee to Christ and followed Him, at the end of our lives when we have this meeting with God, He will say, "The transaction has been completed, and I will give you a greater measure of what you went after on this planet. Heaven is for you."

Conversely, to those who pushed God aside, God will have something else to say. He will say, "You never made the transaction with my Son. I loved you. I sought you. I bought you. I went after you, but you rejected me. You kept your distance from me on earth; you will have a greater measure of this in eternity." We make the choice. God has given us everything we need to believe in Him, but He cannot force us to believe.

THE DECISION

In the first chapter of the book of Romans, Paul tells us that God has littered the universe with clues of His existence. All of creation cries out that there is a God, so much so that those who deny His existence are without excuse: "For since the creation of the world God's invisible qualities—his eternal power and divine nature—have been clearly seen, being understood from what has been made, so that people are without excuse" (Romans 1:20).

Look at the majesty of a mountain range, the placid waters of a forest stream, the intricate features of a newborn child, or the variety, creativity, and color in the flowers of spring. The signs of the Creator are everywhere; they are "clearly seen." Yet some people, in their desperate attempt to deny the existence of God, say that all of this is just an accidental mixing of some organic ingredients in a primordial soup. It is the result of an evolutionary explosion that came out of nowhere, from the hand of no one in particular. There was no first cause because nothing existed until the building blocks of life came into existence. To quote Paul again, many people are exchanging "the truth about God for a lie" (Romans 1:25).

God reveals Himself to us through many different avenues. In addition to His revelation in nature, He has written His laws on our hearts and has revealed Himself to us in His written Word, the Bible. He tugs at our hearts. He elbows us. He whispers in our ears. He convicts us of sin and still so many of us reject Him. How can God throw people into hell? These "good people" have turned their backs on God and in doing so have sealed their own fates.

God is patient, but time will run out. The chances for people to come to Christ will end one day. The Holy Spirit must convict us of sin, but the Bible says He will not strive with us forever. One of the most chilling texts in all of Scripture is Luke 13:25, "Once the owner of the house gets up and closes the door, you will stand outside knocking and pleading, 'Sir, open the door for us.' But he will answer, 'I don't know you or where you come from.'" The picture Christ is painting here is of a person who has burned up all of his chances. If you think you can do your own thing now and become a Christian whenever you want, think again. How long are you going to test the patience of God? I don't know when God gets tired. He doesn't tell us when He closes the door. But one day the door will shut with many people left stranded in the outer darkness.

I do not want you thinking at this point, "All I have to do is bow the knee and say a few magical words, 'Jesus Christ, come into my life.' And, poof, just like that, I have a ticket to heaven." You will miss the train if you think it is that easy. Jesus said, "Not everyone who says to me, 'Lord, Lord,' will enter the kingdom of heaven, but only the one who does the will of my Father who is in heaven. Many will say to me on that day, 'Lord, Lord, did we not prophesy in Your name and in Your name drive out demons and in Your name perform many miracles?' Then I will tell them plainly, 'I never knew you. Away from me, you evildoers!'" (Matthew 7:21-23). We become a Christian by grace through faith. It is God's will, first and foremost, that we place our faith in Christ and His work on the cross. But a lot of people just say the words without really meaning them.

Just before this passage, Jesus said, "Thus, by their fruit you will recognize them" (Matthew 7:20). The sign of authentic faith is action, the fruit of good works. Am I asking you to doubt whether you are a Christ-follower? No. But I am asking you to take inventory. The Christian faith is not some under-the-table deal with God where you can say, "Now I have got a ticket to heaven. I've prayed the prayer. I can do whatever I want and live any way I want. I said the words a long time ago." No, the Christian faith is a relationship. You don't just ask someone if they want to be your friend and then never talk to them. Your friendship is seen through communication and time spent together.

If you have been bought with the blood of Christ, you have nothing to fear. Christ has conquered death. Through our participation by faith in the death and resurrection of Christ, we too can claim the ultimate victory: "'Death has been swallowed up in victory' . . . thanks be to God! He gives us the victory through our Lord Jesus Christ" (1 Corinthians 15:54, 57).

* * *

Take a minute to think of the culture in which we live today. Death is the ultimate threat. The mere idea of death at our doorstep collectively unravels us. What then should we do in the face of such widespread fear in our world today? I find great comfort in knowing death does not have the final word. Christ has victory over sin and death. There is life after. God will make all things new and right all wrongs. We must talk about death and eternity to remind ourselves that we are not all-powerful or in control. We must examine our hearts and ask the question, "Do I really trust God in the face of death? Do I believe the good news of Christ's ultimate victory? Am I afraid of what comes next?" I implore each of you reading this to seriously consider these questions. Instead of denying your mortality, approach it with frankness and humility. Ask God to draw you into His kingdom. We alone cannot save ourselves, but we take comfort in Him, and cling to hope through faith we have received by grace. With Christ alone, if

we give our lives to Him, we have 100 percent assurance that
we will overcome death and live forever with Him in heaven.

Fellowship Creative is the creative and worship team at
Fellowship Church. They wrote a song that regularly reminds
us of the simple truth that death is not the end of our story.
The song is called *"Heaven."* May the lyrics remind you that,
for followers of Jesus, heaven is our greatest hope realized:

In Heaven, Heaven,

It'll only get better in Heaven,

Chains are falling,
Freedom's calling,
Eyes are opened,
Heaven's in motion.

It'll only get better in Heaven!

CHAPTER 7

ANY ROOM FOR GOD?

NO FEAR

Do you love coffee? Most of us do, or at least we know someone who does. How many times have you walked into a coffee shop and the barista says, "You want any room in that coffee?" This is Coffee-ology 101. When they say "room," they're talking about room for half and half, skim milk, almond milk, coconut milk, or any other pollutant we put in our coffee.

It's a great question. A question that we must get vulnerable about in our own lives. The God of the universe is asking you and me that same question when it comes to fear, specifically the fear of God. "Any room? Do you have room in your life for the fear of God?" We have to remember a healthy "fear of God" in the Bible means awe, reverence, and ultimate respect for God. It's putting God in His proper place so perfect love, the love of God, can cast out all earthly fear.

We've talked in depth about the negative and unhealthy fears we all face. We must seek to cast out those fears; they have no place in our lives. But a life of absolutely no fear, devoid of any positive fear or fear of God, would lead to chaos and ruin.

When we live without a fear of God, we are essentially taking a seat on the throne and saying, "I don't need you, I've got this." We become the god of our world, which only leads to destruction.

One of the reasons that we're so sick with the fear virus is that we already have this virus of sin and rebellion influencing every facet of our culture. What's the cause? A lack of the fear of God. What's wrong with our educational system? No fear of God. Our government? No fear of God. Social media and the masters of the universe who run these big platforms? No fear of God. It's a lack of respect and awe of our great God. Why are families falling apart? Why is the divorce rate so high? We've lost the fear of God. Why the crude language? Why the immorality? Why the selfishness? Why are so many people logging onto porn sites? We've lost the fear of God. Why do churches all over our land have to work so hard to get people to show up and to volunteer? We've lost the fear of God.

In our culture, the pendulum has moved from the fear of God and His holiness to "Hey, God is just my friend. He's just like one of my boys. I can live like hell; I can do whatever I want because God loves me. God is all about grace and mercy." That's true. God is a God of mercy and grace. But He's also an awe-inspiring God, a God of wrath and judgment. We've got to find a balance. We have to balance the seesaw between love and fear. Love is not the number one characteristic of God. It's holiness. If I see myself as a sinner in the brilliant blaze of God's holiness, I should have a healthy fear of Him.

If you are the god of your own life and you're running the show, when you come up against the fears in the world, you are going to crumble. Conversely, if God is the God of your life, if Jesus is Lord, when you come up against the fears in the world, you will be able to cast them out through surrendering them to God and dwelling on His love, plan, and sovereignty. It's amazing how we get that inverted and it causes great dysfunction, amplified anxiety, and out-of-control fear in our lives!

Do you have any room for the fear of God? Most of us don't want to make any room because the fear of God doesn't line up with who we want God to be. We want Him to be the benevolent Grandfather, the Amazon Prime God, or the UPS Man—ready to deliver what I want, when I want it. We think God is just here to pour blessings on our life. That's the kind of God we want. In our humanistic, progressive, politically-correct culture—we've forgotten to talk about the fear of God.

I think a lot about the fear of God. I'm not talking about worrying that God is hovering over me with this giant hammer, waiting to whack me. BAM! I'm not saying that. When I say "fear," I'm talking about a 24/7, 360-degree awareness that I'm doing life in front of a holy, just, and almighty God. Every word, thought and action is open before Him and being judged by Him. This may sound scary, but when you invite the fear of God in, you will grow more in your understanding of God's love and sovereignty. You will experience more of His peace and joy.

God loves everyone and He offers forgiveness to everyone. But we have to either receive God's love or reject it. When we turn from our sin and receive His forgiveness, then we will experience how awesome He is as we live under the fear of God. But if we reject Him and choose to do things our own way, then we won't experience His blessing. We will experience a life separated from Him. That is something we should fear.

So often the fear of God drives me to pray for people that I know who don't know Jesus. When I'm with them, the fear of God motivates me to talk to them. If He loves them enough to send me, then I want to fear Him enough to share the gospel with them. Living a life with room for the fear of God leads to the abundant life that Jesus talks about in John 10:10. God wants to give us life to the fullest, and that means a life lived with the fear of God. Living a no-room, no-fear lifestyle leads to destruction, which Jesus talks in depth about in Luke 15.

NO ROOM LIFESTYLE

There is a man mentioned in Luke 15 who had this no-fear, reckless way of life. You might know him as the prodigal son. Through the life of this prodigal son, we see several attributes of this no-fear, reckless, individualistic mentality which says, "I bow to no one. I will chart my own course. I will determine my own destiny."

When we have this kind of no-fear attitude in our lives, we go through four stages with which I think we can all identify. Based on Luke's parable of this infamous biblical free spirit, we are going to identify those stages and relate them to the biblical understanding of the fear of God.

First, let me set the stage of Jesus' story of the prodigal son. The word *prodigal* means "wasteful or reckless and extravagant." Jesus described it this way in Luke 15:13 (NKJV): "And not many days after, the younger son gathered all together, journeyed to a far country, and there wasted his possessions with prodigal living." In other words, this young man burned his inheritance on an all-out hedonistic trip. He tried everything he could until the money ran out. He is remembered as the prodigal son because this kind of wild living characterized his attitude and activity.

The prodigal son was a young man in his teens. It is fairly clear from the lifestyle of his family that he came from a fine Jewish home and had a good father. His older brother was straight as an arrow. Doing what his younger, wilder brother was about to do never occurred to him, as the more responsible son. Our fearless and privileged prodigal son probably attended a Palestine private school, was a three-sport letterman, and was set to share in a decent inheritance.

Everything was going great for him, until one day he became aware of a desire deep within. It was a desire that sounded egotistical, almost evil, but he could not shake it off. He heard this voice echoing in the caverns of his consciousness: "Who is in control of your life? What are you going to do about it? Why don't you break free and do your own thing? Don't let your father and his old-fashioned principles hold you back." At first, he probably resisted following these desires. But day after day, week after week, month after month he heard the voice. The desires that were ringing in the back of his mind soon found their way to the forefront of his mind.

He was losing the moral battle. On one fateful day, he began to obey those desires. He walked up to his father and said: "Dad, give me my inheritance now." His father gave in to his son's wishes. This careless, reckless individual left and went off to the far country to sow his wild oats.

THE DELIRIOUS STAGE

As he began his freefall into sin and recklessness, the prodigal son entered the first stage of a no-fear, godless, and rebellious attitude. This is a stage that we all experience at a certain point in our lives—the delirious stage. You might remember this stage as the first time you came face to face with the simple fact that sin is fun. You probably realized at that time that if sin were not fun, we wouldn't do it. Like the prodigal son, you might have even indulged yourself for a while in the pleasures of sin before realizing the downside to your self-destructive behavior.

This young man was going against the will of his father as well as living in rebellion before God. In his state of delirium, though, he was either unable or unwilling to come to terms with his own rebellion. He was just having too much fun, enthralled with all the excitement, the freshness, and the tantalizing appeal of things he had never experienced before. You know what I am talking about. There is a certain intoxicating feeling of independence when you go your own way and indulge in all the things you've been told for so long that you cannot do.

I had a similar kind of feeling back when I was about sixteen years of age and drove my mother's car alone for the first time. She had a station wagon with a 455 engine beneath the hood. I was driving this big family-mobile all alone down a dirt road with the AM stereo blaring the Bee Gees when I noticed that the sand was kind of loose. The movie *Smokey and the Bandit* had just come out and I wondered if I could do a power slide on that dirt road. I knew deep down that I shouldn't do something like that with my mother's car. But guess what? I went for it and miraculously survived. Thankfully, there was no permanent damage to me or the station wagon. Why did I do it? I felt so free, so independent, and autonomous. The intoxicating feeling beckoned me on, "Come on, Ed, you are in control now. Don't let your mother and her old-fashioned principles hold you back. Do what *you* want."

Maybe you felt that way when you went off to college. As a freshman away from your parents, you could do whatever you wanted to do. Maybe you felt that way the first time you received a bonus check at work. "This is mine. I did it. It's all about me." You went into one of those high-dollar stores and bought the first thing you saw. "I'll take it. I did this. This is all mine now." You felt delirious with excitement.

The prodigal must have felt that way. Friends started coming out of the woodwork. He was buying drinks for them at happy hour. He was wearing designer clothes. Everything was perfect for him. He was the consummate playboy with all the trappings and popularity to go along with his new freedom.

THE DESTRUCTION STAGE

But something happened during this delirious stage. As a result of his reckless and carefree living, he began to get into trouble. Before the prodigal son realized it, the delirious stage was quickly metamorphosing into the second stage: the destruction stage. The Bible says that after we are delirious with excitement and we have experienced those intoxicating feelings of independence, it is just a matter of time before we feel the effects of our self-destruction.

The destruction stage of this young man's life is recorded in Luke 15:14-17. Verse 14 marks the transition into this stage: "After he had spent everything." This young man was trying to leave home to find himself, but he lost himself. He had spent everything. His resources were burnt out. The friends were gone. His clothes were tattered. He was in a heap of trouble. Sin is like that. Sin promises success but ends in failure. Sin promises freedom but delivers slavery. It looks so good and so right, but the destruction phase is brutal.

Verse 14 continues to tell us, "After he had spent everything, there was a severe famine in that whole country, and he began to be in need." Have you ever felt like you were in need relationally, spiritually, or financially? Any one of those needs, on its own, is a tough situation. The prodigal son was experiencing needs on all fronts at the same time. He was at the very lowest point of his life. He was alone. He was spiritually bankrupt and financially wiped out. We are talking about dire need here.

Then, the Bible says this young Jewish man did something

that was detestable, something that was the lowest of the low for a Jew to do: "He went and hired himself out to a citizen of that country, who sent him to his fields to feed pigs" (Luke 15:15). Jews believe that pigs are unclean. Here was the man who had been a playboy with the designer clothes and the flashy jewelry . . . working with pigs. The Bible says that he wanted to eat the pods that were being fed to the pigs. In the mud and the mire of a pig trough, the prodigal had gone rather quickly from the pinnacle to the pit.

Verse 17 of Luke 15 says, "When he came to his senses, he said, 'How many of my father's hired servants have food to spare, and here I am starving to death!'" An empty stomach has a way of preaching to us. He was beginning to smell from the stench of the pigs. He looked at himself and he couldn't believe what he had done. He knew that his father's servants had it better than he did. Jesus said that he "came to his senses." He woke up and smelled the pig slop, so to speak.

The Old Testament writer of Proverbs 14:12 understood well the principle Jesus was trying to get across with this New Testament parable: "There is a way that seems right to a man, but in the end it leads to death" (NHEB). When the prodigal son "came to his senses," he realized that he was dead wrong. He had squandered away his inheritance and lived for a time in reckless abandon because he thought this would give him freedom and independence. He was wrong. It did not give him freedom. Instead, it brought bondage and ruin.

When we try to commandeer our lives and do life apart from God's control, His wisdom, and His expertise, we are thumbing our noses at God. We are jumping into the cockpit, sitting in the captain's seat, white-knuckling the throttle and saying, "God, I am going to fly this plane. Thank you very much, but I don't need any flying lessons. I can fly this baby on my own." When we exhibit that reckless individualistic mentality, it is just a matter of time before we crash. It is not *if*, but *when*. God is standing beside you saying, "Let me fly. I know what's best for you and your life. All you have to do is trust Me."

But we say, "No thanks, God. I know how to handle this marriage problem alone. I know what to do in this dating relationship. I know what to do financially. I know how to invest this money. I know how to move or buy that house. I know what to do all on my own." This is essentially what the prodigal son said as he crashed into the destruction stage of this rebellious lifestyle.

THE DECISION STAGE

The third stage is another that we all go through. Whether outside or inside the family of God, we all experience what I call the decision stage. The prodigal had a choice to make. He had two options. The first option would be for him to say, "I still believe I can do it by myself. I will crawl back into the cockpit of my life. I will sit in the captain's seat again. I will rebuild and fly this plane again."

Then, there's a second option. We can make an assessment

of the situation. We can look at the wreckage and say, "This is nuts. What am I doing? I must come to my senses." This is what the prodigal son did in Luke 15:18, "I will set out and go back to my father and say to him: Father, I have sinned against heaven and against you." He was already rehearsing what he was going to say to his father.

He didn't offer excuses for why he did what he did. He didn't say, "The reason I did this was because I didn't receive counseling as a teenager." He didn't say, "The reason I did this was because I came from a dysfunctional family." He called sin what it was. And then "he got up and went to his father" (Luke 15:20). Some of us need to get up out of that relationship. We need to get up out of that business deal. We need to get up, turn toward God, and come home.

As I rub shoulders with Christians at various places in their journey, I see many people who appear to want God to be the director of their lives. But if the truth were known, beneath the exterior, many of them are not willing to surrender control to God. Their arms are crossed defiantly as they mutter under their breath, "I run this life." If this is you, I challenge you to uncross your arms, to open your palms toward heaven and say, "God, have your way in my life."

THE DELIVERANCE STAGE

All of us, no matter where we are from, go through the first three stages. The fourth stage, though, is only reserved for those who have guts and really want to have Christ enter the picture and deliver them fully, totally, and completely. The fourth stage is the deliverance stage.

If you make the decision to come to your senses, go in the opposite direction of your sinful rebellion, repent, and turn toward the Father, you are in the process of being delivered. Here is where the plot thickens and it really gets exciting. The latter half of Luke 20 reads, "But while he was a long way off, his father saw him." This may seem like an insignificant part of the story, but it is really an amazing testimony to the father's love for his youngest son.

The father had obviously been waiting for his son to return. He had been watching, looking in the distance, and waiting for him to come home. He might have been going up on the rooftop every day for the past couple of years with the slightest hope that he might see his son making his way home again. Perhaps it was his habit to stand at the edge of his property and stare down the road in anticipation of his son's return.

The Bible says he saw him from a distance and that he knew it was his son. How did this old man recognize his son from that far away? I'll tell you how I think he might have recognized him. When I was a teenager, my father was a long way off from me while I was causing trouble with a group of kids. I thought he wouldn't be able to see me, so I wouldn't get in trouble. Suddenly, I heard this voice say, "Ed, come here." I looked up, ran over and asked, "Dad, how did you know it was me?" He said, "By your walk."

In a similar way, I believe the father of the prodigal

recognized his son from a distance. When our heavenly Father sees us take that most difficult first step, He recognizes us at once. "That is my boy. That is my girl. I recognize their stride. They are mine."

The text continues, "His father saw him and was filled with compassion for him." We matter to God even with the mire, the mud, and the crud still stuck to us. You are still a much-loved person by God. But here is the real kicker, the father "ran to his son" (Luke 15:20, emphasis added). The father saw his son from a distance and ran to meet him, to welcome him back. The word "ran" in the Greek language is a powerful, life-changing word. Why is it so significant? It's because Middle Eastern men never ran. It was unheard of for them to run—especially a wealthy, respected, and elderly landowner like this man. Yet this father ran and greeted his son.

Luke 15:20 also says that he embraced his son: "He ran to his son, threw his arms around him and kissed him." The law, specifically in the book of Deuteronomy, demanded that this young man, this prodigal, no-fear-bearing individualist who took the trust fund and squandered it on reckless living, should have been stoned by the neighbors. If the neighbors, though, stoned the son, they would have had to stone the father as well. Why? The father was just as culpable because the father was embracing the son and welcoming a sinner back home.

What a picture of what Jesus did for us on the cross. He embraced us. He took the licks. He took the hit for our sins. He is a compassionate, loving, and gracious God who wants to know us, relate to us, lift us up in His arms, and draw us near to Him.

The Bible then says that they had a giant party. The prodigal son was trying to get his rehearsed confession out. "Dad, I have sinned against you. I am sorry." His father, though, had already forgiven him and was ready to celebrate his return.

Here is how Jesus describes the father's response to his son's homecoming, beginning in verse 22 and continuing through verse 24: "But the father said to his servants, 'Quick! Bring the best robe and put it on him.'" Only family members wore robes. "Put a ring on his finger." Only a family member could wear the family signet ring, the power of attorney, that was used to seal documents. "And sandals on his feet." Only family members wore shoes. If you were a slave, you didn't wear shoes. "'Bring the fattened calf and kill it. Let's have a feast and celebrate. For this son of mine was dead and is alive again; he was lost and is found.' So they began to celebrate."

You might be thinking, "You mean this father put on this kind of party for the son who rebelled against him, who had done his own thing and wasted his inheritance?" Yes, that is the kind of party that God wants to throw for us when we turn back to Him. But, again, we are back to the issue of consequence. We are back to the issue of confronting our no-fear mentality. If you are honest with yourself, you may find that even though you are forgiven, you are paying high tabs for this mentality that says, "I'll do my own thing."

You may be paying high tabs relationally, because you have been through a marriage or two. These, in turn, may have brought about negative consequences for a child or two.

Maybe you have bought into the lie that more is better when it comes to finances, but you are up to your eyeballs in debt. Even still, He loves you more than you can even comprehend. He is waiting for you to make just a little move, just one step toward home so He can come running to greet you, save you, change you, and restore you to His family. You can wear His robe, put on His ring, and wear His shoes. But the choice is up to you. Isn't it time to come home? Home is where you will find healing. Home is where you will find hope. Home is where you will be cared for by the hands of your heavenly Father. It all begins with a healthy fear of God. So, again, I ask you the question: "Any room?"

CHAPTER 8

THE GREAT PHYSICIAN

FEAR OF GOD

It's about six in the morning, and I'm at the hospital getting ready for heart surgery. I'm upbeat and looking forward to getting it over with. They prep me for surgery, put me on the gurney, and wheel me into the operating room.

I feel confident because, after all, I have Dr. Gerald Lawrie performing the surgery. I had recently found out that he's operated on emperors, kings and queens, heads of state, and celebrities. I'm thinking "I'm in good hands." Though, ultimately, my life is in the best Hands of all.

No matter the outcome of the surgery, I trust Christ with my life. I fear Him and Him alone. Do I have some "what if" scenarios come to mind? Sure! "What if I don't wake up? What if the surgery is not a success?" But in the end, I choose to trust my heavenly Father. God loves my family more than I ever could. I can trust Him with them and everything else that is precious to me. I have nothing to fear because He is the only

One I fear. I slowly lose consciousness and the surgery begins.

Three months later, I am sitting in Dr. Lawrie's office and we are talking about the success of my surgery. He reminds me of where I had come from, "Had you not had surgery, you would have become sicker and sicker. Within six to twelve months, it could've been over." Fortunately, I had asked Dr. Lawrie to intervene, and he saved my life.

When the Bible refers to God as the Great Physician, it is emphasizing God's desire and expertise in healing human hearts. We are broken, beyond human repair from sin, but the Great Physician takes what is broken and makes it whole. We are all heart patients, and I want to pray the heart patient's prayer with you. Did you know that this prayer is in the Bible? It is Psalm 139:23-24, "Search me, God, and know my heart; test me and know my anxious thoughts. See if there is any offensive way in me and lead me in the way everlasting."

Search me. Test me. See me. Lead me.

That is the heart patient's prayer. I'm going to challenge you right now to put yourself on the operating table, God's operating table. Get off the gurney, walk up to the operating table, and lay yourself bare before God. We're all going to discover things in our lives we never knew were there. We are going to root out the fear virus and figure out: What's driving that anger in your life? What's the real source of those fears you carry? What's causing those insecurities? God is also going to pinpoint sin that needs to be addressed.

The surgeon is the Savior, the scalpel is Scripture, and the heart is the hope and home of Jesus. My heart is made for Jesus and so is yours. My heart is my hope and it should be Christ's home. We know that the heart is the seat of self and it is who we really are. It's the essence of our morals and ethics. When we accept Jesus as our Lord and we give the totality of our lives to Him, there's a heart transplant that takes place. Maybe you've not experienced that yet. You need to know what's out there when you choose to have this surgery.

So, let's talk about this surgery only God can perform. When Dr. Lawrie looked at me and told me what to expect, what if I would have said to him, "I'm not going to do it. Who are you? I know my heart; I feel fine Dr. Lawrie." I would have been a card-carrying idiot! However, how often in my own life have I said, "God, I know what's best for me, I'm going to follow my heart on this deal"? Well, let's be smart and listen to our Great Physician. Allow God to walk us through surgery as we read through these four, two-word prayers. Search me. Test me. See me. Lead me.

SEARCH ME

The first two-word prayer is "Search me" and it was written during a time of great struggle and tribulation by David in the Old Testament. David was called a man after God's own heart. Though he was definitely not perfect, David shows us how to come to the One who is perfect and humbly ask for help. The Bible says, in Psalm 139:23, "Search me, God, and know my heart."

Let me say it again: only God knows our heart. We think

we know ourselves—and we do to a certain degree—but we don't really know ourselves apart from God. For example, *search me* literally means "to crack open, to dig deep, to cut." We ask God to help us search ourselves as we get open and vulnerable before Him. David was bold and courageous from a young age and as a shepherd, he killed a lion and a bear in defense of his father's sheep. He then went on to slay the big behemoth Goliath. But this prayer of Psalm 139 had to be one of his most courageous acts. This prayer was a plea and invitation for God to search his innermost heart and feelings. He was completely vulnerable before God.

Are you courageous enough to pray that? I promise if you do, great things will happen. You will grow in your faith, understanding, wisdom, acceptance of yourself and others, peace, confidence, and trust in God's goodness. The list goes on and on. Painful things will also occur. You will become aware of things that need to change and you will most likely need to process past pains so you can begin the road to healing.

We have to know God's not going to be surprised by anything we are going to reveal to Him. God's not going to say, "Oh, I had no idea! Oh, really, you have that issue? Wow, I didn't know that." God knows everything, yet we have to say, "God, you know me. Search me and know my heart."

The problem with the heart is the heart of the problem. Look around our world today. Mankind, left to its own devices, will do extremely dark things. However, we have great potential for good when Jesus comes into our lives. Now is the time to say, "Search me God, dig deep into me and uncover what is holding me back from Your success. Show me opportunities to grow in my faith and thrive in every area of life. Open my eyes to any and all hypocrisy that I have. Lord, bring into the light any part of my life that rejects Your authority or is in conflict with the truth of Your Word. Reveal to me any area of my heart, mind, and soul that does not fully trust You, and help me change."

TEST ME

"Test me." That's the next two-word prayer. Oh, I've had a lot of tests, I can tell you that. They all came out with the same answer, "You have a major problem with your heart." God is also going to test you and me to expose potential heart issues we may have. We have stress tests in life designed to show us what is really housed in our hearts. This process is not easy, but it's necessary if we are going to become everything God has destined us to be. We need to willingly present ourselves to Him and say, "God perform a stress test on me. Test me and know my anxious thoughts."

When we are stressed and pressed, something will always come out. Hopefully, what we see pour out of our hearts through testing will be love, joy, peace, patience, kindness, goodness, faithfulness, gentleness, and self-control (Galatians 5:22-23). This is the character of Christ and it's impossible to consistently produce without relying on Jesus daily. However, if you are like me, you do not always reflect these character qualities. Too often, our anxious and fearful thoughts drive our actions and decisions. Sometimes things come out of our hearts that don't line up with that list of character traits. It's in the testing that we see how we have grown and the places we still need continued improvement.

How does God build character? He tests us. Maybe you have a problem with being impatient. He's going to put you in situations that build your patience and they're not going to be easy. Maybe you have a problem with anger and volatility. He's going to put you in a situation to build your self-control. Maybe you have a pride problem and you don't realize that you are running on fumes from all of the self-reliance and self-centeredness. He's going to push you to your limit so you recognize your need for Him. It may be that when you were praying for help, the loving answer God gave you was a test designed to help you change.

SEE ME

The third two-word prayer is "See me." Only God can really see what's in our lives. Psalm 139:24 says, "And see if there is any wicked way in me" (NKJV). This phrase "wicked way," is literally translated from the original language as "forced labor."

What do we say in our world today? "Oh, I'm just going to go with my heart. I'm going to follow my heart. I'm going to be free." As we follow our heart and it leads us into so called "freedom," the things we choose to do will eventually incarcerate and imprison us. We begin to work for this newfound freedom, and it brings pain and suffering; it's forced labor and we don't even realize it! We're working for it and completely enslaved to it. Some of us are in forced labor right now because of lust and pornography. Some of us are in forced labor and chained up because of greed. Some of us are in forced labor because of rebellion against authority figures in our lives who are there to guide and protect us. I am telling you this not to judge you, but to help you. God is saying to you and me, "Life is too short to be a slave to sin, and only Jesus can free you!"

Again, Jeremiah 17:9 tells us, "The heart is deceitful above all things, and desperately wicked; Who can know it?" (NKJV). The answer is God. He knows our condition and desires to help us with our heart sickness. Only God can know because we are so easily self-deceived by our own heart. Do you know how sinister this sin is that we carry? Sin has the ability to hide itself from us. Sin has the ability to camouflage our depravity, our disease, and our debauchery. We need God's help just to be honest with Him and ourselves.

Only God can say "Ed, look at that. Hey, check that darkness out. Wow, that's coming to the surface; we need to deal with that." At first, it is painful to process our sin, shortcomings, and self-centeredness before God. But if we confess it, which means we tell the truth about it before God, then we can begin to experience the forgiveness and peace found in Christ. The Master Surgeon is our Savior, the scalpel is His Word, and He will cut deep through any deception.

LEAD ME

"Search me, oh God, and know my heart. Test me and know my anxious thoughts. And see if there is any wicked way in me…and lead me in the way everlasting." " I love this last two-word prayer found at the end of Psalm 139:24.

"Lead me."

If we just follow our heart, our heart will lead us to hell. God wants to transform your heart and give you a new heart that is quick to follow His leadership path for your life. Are you going God's way? Are you on His path for you?

Maybe you're a student in junior high, high school, or college. Maybe you're starting a new adventure at work. Maybe you just realized, "I've been following my heart in this dating relationship as opposed to allowing God to say, 'Here's what I want for you.' Which way are you going to go? Who will you follow? God's road is always better. God's way is always better than your way or my way. He's the Master Surgeon. In Mark 2:17, we read, "Jesus said to them, 'It is not the healthy who need a doctor, but the sick. I have not come to call the righteous, but sinners.'"

The scalpel is the Scripture. Check this out. Hebrews 4:12-14, "His powerful Word is sharp as a surgeon's scalpel, cutting through everything, whether doubt or defense, laying us open to listen and obey. Nothing and no one is impervious to God's Word. We can't get away from it—no matter what" (MSG). When you run away from God, you'll always run right into Him. And He is willing to do surgery in your life and in your heart. In Ezekiel 36:26 God says to us, "I will give you a new heart, and I will put a new spirit in you" (MSG). But He will not force you because He is looking for a willing patient who will submit themselves to His care.

Dr. Lawrie told me something that freaked me out after surgery. He said, "Because your heart had been stopped, and because air gets in it, we took your heart and massaged it." He went on to explain, "I touched your heart and massaged it for five minutes and then we tested it to make sure it was healthy. Finally, we closed you up and you were on your way to ICU recovery. Had I not massaged it," he said, "you probably would have stroked out." He touched my heart!

There is a Master Surgeon and He's the only One who can touch your heart and mine. His name is Jesus. Have you given Him your life? Have you said, "Jesus, have your way with me"? Maybe you've never prayed that prayer to give your heart to Him. You can do it right now. Let God touch your heart because that's what an open heart is all about.

Here's how Jesus can transform your heart. It's as easy as ABC:

- **ADMIT** that you're a sinner, that you have the virus of sin, that you are living a life that is falling short of God's standards.
- **BELIEVE** that Jesus died on the cross for your sins and rose again.
- **CONFESS** that Jesus Christ is your Lord and Savior and commit to following Him.

You simply say, "Jesus, I admit to you that I'm a sinner. I believe to the best of my ability that you died for my sins and rose again, and I confess that you are my Lord and I want you, Jesus, to lead every area of my life. Thank you for forgiving me and for this new life I have in You." If you prayed that prayer, that's the greatest thing that you'll ever do.

Some of you have already given your life to Christ but you either realize you need to make changes or know something is not right in your relationship with Him. Here's how you can rededicate your life to Jesus. It's also as easy as ABC:

- **ASK** God to search you, test you, and reveal what is holding you back from His success in your life, and lead you in submitting every area of your life to Him.
- **BELIEVE** that Jesus died and rose again not only to pay for your sin debt but also to break the power of sin that causes you to reject Christ's leadership.
- **CHOOSE** to rely on Christ daily to help you make changes, trust Him, and obey Him as you are powerless to do so on your own.

You simply say, "Jesus, I ask you to search me, test me, see me revealing what is holding me back from Your success in my life and lead me in submitting every area of my life to you. I believe you died for me and rose again to break the power of sin over me. I choose to rely on You, Jesus, as I am powerless on my own. Help me make the necessary changes and fully trust and obey You today."

* * *

After surgery, it is important to take good care of yourself as you recover. After my heart surgery, I had to take things easy for a while: dietary changes, no strenuous activity, and plenty of sleep. In our relationship with God, after we have given over every part of our heart to Him, we can't just forget that the transformation ever happened. We have to live in light of it every day, taking care of ourselves and nurturing our relationship with God. We do this through understanding more of who God is and that He is worthy of fear.

GOD'S RIGHTFUL PLACE

The Bible says, "There is no fear in love. But perfect love drives out fear, because fear has to do with punishment. The one who fears is not made perfect in love" (1 John 4:18). The kind of fear that John is talking about in this verse relates to the other fears I have been talking about up to this point. This is an irrational, earthly fear—fear of the future, of commitment, of failure. It also speaks of an irrational fear of God, a fear of God's judgment without an understanding of God's perfect love. In order to understand what it means to fear God in a biblical sense, we must understand who God is and how much He loves us.

We need to identify God as God. We need to recognize Him as the Sovereign Lord of the universe. The Bible has many different names for God because each name identifies a different aspect of God. These names are important because they communicate to God that we are seeking to know Him and to build a relationship with Him. God does not need us to tell Him who He is. We need to reinforce in our own lives who God is in relation to us. God is not suffering an identity crisis. He is not saying, "I did not realize I was God. Thanks for telling me. I did not know I made the heavens and the earth. I am so glad you reminded me that I sent my Son to die on the cross for the sins of the world. Thanks for sharing." No, God does not need this recognition, but we need to recognize Him. When I regularly recognize who God is, my pride and ego begin to melt, and I realize that He is God and I am not.

The fear of God is not cowering or tucking your tail between your legs and running away. It is, first of all, recognizing who God is and coming to know His character as revealed to us in His Word. He wants us to know Him and to recognize His power, but He does not want us quaking in our boots with an impulsive desire to run in the other direction. Our reverence for God should draw us to Him and build in us a desire to understand better where we stand in relation to Him.

I have to remind myself daily that I am a sinner and I will go south if left unchecked. If I do not regularly recognize who God is, if I do not give Him that significant slot in my life, I begin to think I am God—ruling over a universe called Me. A lot of people I meet these days think they are God. They may not say it, but they do not regularly recognize who God is. They think things like, "I call the shots. I have pulled myself up by my own bootstraps. I have made the money. I am in charge. I will determine my own destiny. I will forge my own future." We must recognize who God is and look at His attributes that, when balanced with a fear of Him, lead us to a flourishing spiritual life. Then and only then will we begin to have a healthy fear of God and be able to discern the balance between love and fear, the relationship between trust and fear, and the connection between obedience and fear.

A BALANCING ACT

Certain things are inseparably linked in our culture: money and professional athletes, chocolate chips and cookies, pandemics and not touching your face, just to name a few. Another pair is love and fear in the Bible. Psalm 33:18 reads, "But the eyes of the Lord are on those who fear him, on those whose hope is in His unfailing love." Psalm 118:4 also tells us, "Let those who fear the Lord say: 'His love endures forever.'" Fear and love are part of the balanced equation of God's unchanging character. If you emphasize one over the other, you do not have an accurate or healthy image of God.

Many of us don't recognize who God is, and we don't recognize the critical balance between fear and love. If we fall too far on the fear side, we become legalistic. Christianity becomes nothing but rituals and regulations. We sometimes are tempted to think, "I must jump through this hoop, I must do this and do that, or else God might hit me with a heavenly hammer."

Remember, Christianity is not a guilt trip; it is a relationship.

On the other hand, we can get so far out of balance on the love side that we take too many liberties with God. We think since God loves us unconditionally, it does not matter how we live. Yes, God does love us unconditionally, but His judgment is tethered to His love. We must understand our fear of God is a critical component of our love for Him. We should obey Him because we love Him, but a part of that love is a fearful realization that God is an awesome and powerful judge who will hold us accountable for our actions. If we fall too far on the side of love and liberty, we can become lackadaisical about our Christian commitment.

From making time for private prayer, to corporate worship, to trusting God with your bank account, to balancing evangelism with social action, you may be convicted of many areas of imbalance in your life. But as you trust God, casting aside all other fears, and begin to choose His path, you will experience the peace and satisfaction of being firmly rooted in the things of God:

> *He will be like a tree planted by the water*
> *that sends out its roots by the stream. It*
> *does not fear when heat comes; its leaves*
> *are always green. It has no worries in a*
> *year of drought and never fails to bear fruit.*
> *(Jeremiah 17:8)*

A TRUSTWORTHY GOD

When Moses was at the base of Mount Sinai after receiving the Ten Commandments, this is what he communicated to the children of Israel in Exodus 20:20: "Do not be afraid. God has come to test you, so that the fear of God will be with you to keep you from sinning." Moses said, "Do not be afraid but fear God." What kind of double-talk is that? How can fear keep you from being afraid? And how can it keep you from sinning?

What God was saying through Moses was that we should fear nothing else but God. Our love and fear of Him will cast out all other fears. Only God is worthy of our awe, respect, reverence, and obedience. When we worship and fear God, nothing else can touch us. When we understand and connect with God's awesome power, we will be motivated not to sin against Him.

Despite their many warnings and the awesome power of God displayed in their lives time and again, the children of Israel rebelled many times. They disobeyed God and His law repeatedly. They fell into idolatry, drunkenness, and a multitude of other sins. They paid a price for their disobedience. The death sentence of idolaters at the foot of Mount Sinai, the wilderness wanderings, the delayed entrance into the Promised Land, the tumultuous times of the judges, oppression by the enemies of Israel—all these were the results of disobedience. When the fear of God was absent, the fear of everything was present. Their fear of God represented trust, and without that trust they had many enemies and hardships to fear.

The law God handed down to Moses was intended to keep Israel pure, to protect them, and to pave the way for the promised Messiah. Out of love, He gave them the law; out of love, He disciplined them for breaking it. The fear of God will keep you from sinning as you begin to recognize that God's love drives His will for our lives.

GOD'S GAME PLAN

Fear of God is about a willingness to go by God's game plan. It is a willingness to obey, to trust God and do what He says. Solomon, one of the most powerful men to rule over ancient Israel, discovered this important principle too late in life. He was David's heir to the throne, the builder of God's temple, the wisest and the richest of kings. I call Solomon "Solo Man" because he tried to do it his way. For forty years, Solomon tasted power, pleasures, and possessions like we will never experience.

If Solomon constructed his house today, it would probably cost billions of dollars. He had seven hundred wives. He wrote thousands of proverbs. He was the toast of the town, the man of the hour, the tower of mighty Israelite power. Laymen and leaders alike traveled from far and wide to seek out the wisdom he possessed. Seemingly, he had it all.

Near the end of his life, though, "Solo Man" had many regrets about the years he had spent in hedonistic revelry apart from the will of God. It was during these later years that he wrote the often bitter and sardonic words found in the Book of Ecclesiastes. After burning up four decades of his life, he looked back in the rearview mirror and penned these words in Ecclesiastes 12:13, which are still relevant for us today: "Now all has been heard; here is the conclusion of the matter: Fear God and keep his commandments, for this is the duty of all mankind."

Solomon had done it all. There isn't a better test case for what it is like to try to live apart from God, surrounded by all the pleasures of the world. But after all he had done, possessed, and enjoyed, here was his final conclusion, the net effect of his experiential wisdom: "Fear God and keep his commandments." That, he said, is the entirety of man's duty to God. This is the sum total of all that God requires of us.

God preserved the words, thoughts, and journeys of Solomon so we wouldn't have to take the same meaningless journey that he did in order to come to the same conclusion. Don't spend your life trying all the things the world has to offer, only to come to the end of it filled with regret and bitterness. Take Solomon's word for it now, while you still have the opportunity to redeem the time. Fear God and obey Him; that is the conclusion of the matter.

Are you going by God's game plan? God wants willing warriors. He wants people who say, "God, I want to do it your way. I'm not going to be a little god sovereignly ruling over a universe called Me. You are God. I am not. You have the game plan for me that is the best. My life will hit on all cylinders when I fear you and obey you. I want to do what you want me to do."

We don't know what to do unless we know God's game plan.

God's game plan is revealed to us in the Bible. The Christian life works when we follow the playbook. Christianity teaches us the plays we need in order to navigate skillfully through the twists and turns of our messed-up culture.

You might be saying to yourself, "I thought I was in the game, but I have never made a commitment to God and agreed to play by His game plan." Christianity is a decision followed by a process. Compare the Christian commitment, for example, to being married. You don't just wake up one day and say, "Oh, I'm married. I can't believe it. How did that happen?" Any single person can tell you that it is not that easy. You have to come to a point where you say, "I do." But it doesn't end there; there is a process after that commitment.

THE COSTS AND BENEFITS

When I got heart surgery, it cost me. I had to prepare for surgery and recover from surgery. It was not easy; it took a lot out of me. But getting surgery benefitted me way more than what it cost me. Surgery saved my life, and I am so grateful that I am alive today and able to spend more time with my family.

Deciding to live in a way that makes room for the fear of God in your life will cost you some things. It is not always easy. It is hard to surrender control to God, to trust Him and be obedient to Him even when we don't feel like it. The gospel of Jesus Christ is the essence of simplicity, but commitment to Him and the continuing process of following Him will take everything you have.

But the benefits of deciding to make room for the fear of God in your life are unparalleled. When you surrender all fear to God, give Him complete control of your life and walk out your relationship with Him daily, you will experience the benefits of a healthy fear of God: direction, compassion, blessings, contentment, and maturity. These are things God offers to those who fear him.

1. DIRECTION

We read in Psalm 25:12, "Who, then, are those who fear the Lord? He will instruct them in the ways they should choose." As we give God His proper place in our lives, we will be more in tune with how God wants us to live. When we begin to trust Him and deepen our relationship with Him, He will make our paths straight.

Have you ever said, "I just don't know what to do?" There have been many times in my life when I did not know which road to take, when I could not see what lay around the bend. But I know the One who does have all the answers, and He wants to share those answers with me. All He asks of me is that I submit to Him.

Christian commitment has no place for pride. God is a jealous God, and He wants all of our devotion. And when we give it to Him, He rewards us by guiding and directing us in ways we never thought possible. The assurance of this kind of guidance from an all-knowing, all-powerful, and omnipresent God should bring us peace of mind. It should chase away any other fears or worries we have in life. We are riding on God's shoulders now, and He has promised to show us the way.

2. COMPASSION

When we fear God, we are also assured of His compassion. Psalm 103:13 says, "As a father has compassion on his children, so the Lord has compassion on those who fear him." When we make the commitment to Christ by faith, we are adopted into the family of God. We become God's children. The Apostle Paul tells us that we become coheirs with Christ and share in all of the spiritual rights and benefits afforded to such status.

One of those benefits is the unending compassion of our heavenly Father. God shows compassion to the entire world, as evidenced by sending His Son to die for the sins of the world. For His children, God's mercy is unending. Jeremiah speaks of his great hope in the compassion of God toward His people, "Yet this I call to mind and therefore I have hope: Because of the Lord's great love we are not consumed, for his compassions never fail. They are new every morning; great is your faithfulness" (Lamentations 3:21-23).

This is the hope of everyone who is called a child of God—that God's mercy will never fail us. Because Christ has already suffered the judgment we deserved, God's justice has been satisfied and His mercy is ours forever.

3. BLESSINGS

The blessings of God toward those who fear Him are many. Proverbs 22:4 lists some of them: "The rewards of humility and fear of the Lord are riches, honor, and life" (NASB). God has no tolerance for pride, but He rewards humility in both tangible and spiritual ways. Godly fear should bring us to a place of humility before the awesome person of God.

When we commit our lives to God and recognize who He is, we are humbling ourselves before Him. God is a great rewarder of those who live in humility. But the difficult part of humility is that if you think you have it, you probably don't. If you are trying to manufacture Christian humility in order to receive God's blessings, you probably will not find true humility.

Christ taught His disciples the way of humility: "Whoever wants to become great among you must be your servant, and whoever wants to be first must be slave of all. For even the Son of Man did not come to be served, but to serve, and to give His life as a ransom for many." (Mark 10:43-45). It is in service to God and others that we become great in God's kingdom. Only in selfless sacrifice, thinking of others before yourself, and making the mind of Christ your own will you find true humility.

Paul also talks about this kind of humility in a wonderful passage in Philippians 2, which describes the selfless attitude of Christ Jesus. This passage is believed to be a familiar hymn of the early church:

> *Your attitude should be the same as*
> *that of Christ Jesus: Who, being in very*
> *nature God, did not consider equality*
> *with God something to be used to His*
> *own advantage; rather, He made himself*

nothingby taking the very nature of a
servant, being made in human likeness.
And being found in appearance as a man,
He humbled himself by becoming obedient
to death—even death on a cross!
Therefore God exalted Him to the highest
place and gave Him the name that is above
every name, that at the name of Jesus
every knee should bow, in heaven and
on earth and under the earth,and every
tongue acknowledge that Jesus Christ is
Lord, to the glory of God the Father.
(Philippians 2:5-11)

If you want the riches, honor, and abundant life that God promises, don't look for them. Instead, look for ways to put on the same attitude that Christ had by being a willing and obedient servant. You take care of the obedience part; God will take care of the rewards. By seeking first place, you will be last in God's economy. But by seeking to be last and putting other's needs before your own, you will have first place.

4. CONTENTMENT

The idea of being content—satisfied with what one has—is a foreign concept in today's world. There is no end to the list of things that we can attain and acquire in life, but very few of these things do we actually need. Psalm 34:9-10 gives us the key to contentment: "Fear the Lord, you His holy saints, for those who fear him lack nothing. The lions may grow weak and hungry, but those who seek the Lord lack no good thing."

How does the fear of the Lord bring contentment? It is all about priorities. When God has first place in our lives and we have put nothing else in front of Him, He satisfies our every need because He is all we need.

The new car loses its luster and the new home does not impress anymore. The dream vacation, the jewelry, the clothes, the portfolio of stocks—none of these can compare to the incomparable riches which are ours in Christ Jesus (Ephesians 2:7). Godly fear gives us a perspective in life that few people are able to have because it gives us God's eternal perspective on all we do and all we have. Temporal and material things slip in importance when viewed through eternal eyes.

The fear of the Lord also helps us become content because we know that everything we have belongs to God. God has given us just what we need to live, enjoy life, and be able to give generously. We understand that all we have is God's anyway, and we are accountable to God for how we use the resources He has entrusted into our care. Instead of hoarding or spending what we earn on frivolous desires, we use our resources to further God's Kingdom.

In Philippians 4:12-13, Paul wrote: "I have learned the secret of being content in any and every situation, whether well fed or hungry, whether living in plenty or in want. I can do all this through Him who gives me strength." Paul's focus was on Christ. He realized that regardless of his financial situation or even where his next meal was coming from, Christ was his security. That is the bottom line of contentment. Where does your security come from? Paul's security came from his faith in Christ and the knowledge that through famine, prison, beatings, and many other hardships, Christ would be his all in all.

When you truly understand who God is and the significance of the relationship you have through Christ, you will know where real contentment lies. The world cannot offer this type of contentment. Neither can any other religious leader or system. Only Christ brings lasting, eternal peace and contentment.

5.   MATURITY

A final benefit to the fear of God is maturity. Over a lifetime of trusting God, revering Him, and submitting to His will, we grow into the spiritual maturity that the New Testament calls "sanctification of the believer." This is the process of walking with Christ after making a faith commitment to Him. As we follow Christ, we become more and more like Him until we win the prize of maturity, the perfection of the saints. Paul described this prize in the book of Philippians:

> *Not that I have already obtained all this, or*
> *have already arrived at my goal, but I press*
> *on to take hold of that for which Christ*
> *Jesus took hold of me. Brothers and sisters,*
> *I do not consider myself yet to have taken*
> *hold of it. But one thing I do: Forgetting*
> *what is behind and straining toward what*
> *is ahead, I press on toward the goal to*

win the prize for which God has called me
heavenward in Christ Jesus
(Philippians 3:12-14).

We will not attain real perfection, of course, until we reach heaven. But Paul is clear that we should press toward this goal and reach for the prize of maturity even in this lifetime. Fearing God brings us closer to the goal as we forge a deeper relationship with Him.

* * *

In Matthew 11:28-30 Jesus said, "Come to me, all you who are weary and burdened, and I will give you rest. Take my yoke upon you and learn from me, for I am gentle and humble in heart, and you will find rest for your souls. For my yoke is easy and my burden is light." God is the Great Physician who can bear all of our worry, and in exchange, He gives us blessing upon blessing.

Fear is the most basic instinct of all creatures. Humans, most of all, have created a myriad of fears, anxieties, worries, cares, and phobias to plague our lives. It is certainly an understatement to say that we know fear. And it is only in fearing God—through faith in Him, hope in His promises, and an understanding of His love—that we can truly overcome our earthly fears. When you fear God, you have nothing left to fear, not even fear itself.

CHAPTER 9

THE VACCINE

FREEDOM FROM FEAR

One night, I walked outside in our driveway and I saw in the shadow what looked like an alien creature. As I looked closer, it was a magnificent beetle. I think it's called an emperor beetle. He was just making his way across our driveway and he had an attitude! He was big—you could see the biceps and the triceps of this bug. He was walking with major swagger, all of his legs moving in cadence. So, I thought, "I'm going to go face to face with this beetle." I don't know why I did it, but I did. I got down on his level and I just looked at the beetle. Have you ever stared into the eyes of a beetle? This beetle was massive. This bug looked like he was going to walk right into my face. He was not veering to the right or to the left.

I got up, got a little stick, picked him up, put him back in the grass, and he went on his merry way. That beetle didn't know he was messing with a human being, did he? From his perspective he was totally free to do what he wanted to do, where he wanted to do it. He didn't know that he was facing someone that owned the lot he was on, that owned the driveway, that owned the house. He was just a beetle, a little beetle-brain insect. Yet he'd come face to face with this human being, this force, this person much bigger, much greater, much more powerful than his little brain could capture.

How often do we do the same thing? In our beetle-esque mentality we come face to face with God and we don't realize how powerful, how awesome, how amazing He is. We just think, "You know what? I'm going to walk the way I'm going to walk. I'm going to walk across my driveway because this is my yard, this is my house, this is my marriage, this is my life, this is my career, and these are my abilities. I'm going to do what I want to do." We don't realize we're doing it right in front of God—the One who created us and who really owns everything.

Living in the fantasy of our own greatness is not freedom. Living in the reality of God's infinite greatness is what will give us the humble view of ourselves that leads to life-transforming freedom. Our great God is omnipresent. That means He is everywhere. There's no place where God is not. Not only is God omnipresent, He is omniscient. He knows everything. He knows everything in the past, present, and future. You're not going to surprise God. You're not going to shock Him. He knows it all, all at once.

Have you ever heard the phrase "God Almighty"? It's in the Bible 345 times. It is declaring that God is omnipotent. That phrase simply means He's all-powerful. We so often forget about the power of God. We're like the beetle. We forget who it is we're facing and who it is we're trying to negotiate with. We act like we have confidence, then one day we encounter a circumstance and situation that is bigger than us. It demands a solution that is greater than what we can produce on our own. The façade is shattered, and we realize that we cannot face the challenge in front of us on our own.

That was the point all along: we were never meant to face life on our own. The Bible tells us that this Almighty God, in the person of Jesus Christ, has come to live inside us to empower us daily to be all that God has destined us to be. However, so many of us are working very hard at trying to live self-empowered and apart from God when our only chance at success is to place our hope fully in Him!

Our attitude of self-sufficiency seems to be working out for us in seasons of plenty when there are no obstacles in our path. But when something comes in and knocks us off course—like when I moved the beetle into the grass—we begin to feel like we are drowning and hopeless. The control we felt we had vanishes.

If we were to take a survey today and everyone responded with complete honesty and candor, I believe we would discover that many feel as though they are in hopeless situations. You may be one of those people. You may feel hopeless about a marriage that is not getting better. You may feel hopeless because you are not yet married and don't have any prospects in the foreseeable future. Maybe you are a husband or wife that feels hopeless because you don't have a child yet. Or maybe you have a sense of hopelessness because of a difficulty at work, a financial setback, or a debilitating illness.

In the midst of all the fears we are likely to face in this

lifetime, hopelessness is a pervasive condition in the world today. But the Bible gives us the secret for being hopeful. The secret is revealed to us in a little book called Colossians. In Colossians 1:26-27, Paul says that a mystery has been hidden for all ages but has now been revealed. And this mystery, this secret, is revealed to the saints of God, even the Gentiles: "Christ in you, the hope of glory." Note the phrase "in you." If we are in Christ, Jesus gives us the reason for hope. This is precisely why: if you are a Christ-follower, you should be among the most confident and most hopeful people on the planet.

How do I have hope that never hides? When our fears seem to engulf us and we can't seem to find a reason for hope, how do we tap into that source of hope that lives inside us as Christ-followers? The Bible says in Colossians 1:27 that hope is a person. Because of the unfailing character of the person of Christ, we can be confident that what He says and what He promises will actually happen. That is biblical, honest-to-goodness, Holy Spirit-inspired hope. Do you have that kind of hope?

Every time I think about hope, my mind rushes back to an occasion years ago when Lisa and I were planning a mission trip to Korea. This trip was really exciting for us, but we were hesitant about leaving. Our oldest daughter LeeBeth was only three years old at the time and we had not been away from her for an extended period of time. We decided to make the trip and entrusted LeeBeth into the loving care of relatives. We kissed her goodbye and hugged her, and Lisa got a little teary at the prospect of leaving her little girl for two weeks.

As we turned to walk toward the car that was taking us to the airport, LeeBeth said, "Mommy, Daddy, please bring me back a Korean outfit." Now is that classic, or what? This is the typical toddler response when mommy and daddy leave for a trip: "Bring me back a present."

We promised that we would try our best to do just that. We went to the airport, hopped on a plane, and made it safely to Korea. We spent two incredible weeks there and then made our way back. When we pulled the car in front of the house and walked up the walkway, the door flew open, LeeBeth ran out, jumped into our arms, kissed us, and said she was glad we were home. Then, without missing a beat, she said, "Put me down. Put me down." We did as she asked, and she immediately began to take off her clothes. We were startled and asked why she was taking off her clothes.

She responded excitedly, "Where is my new outfit?" We unbuckled our suitcases, took out the Korean outfit, gave it to her, and she put it on. Now that is hope! She was confident in what she expected to happen because her hope had been placed in her mommy and daddy who promised it would happen.

We should aspire to be like LeeBeth when it comes to hope and the expectation that we have in God. We must place our hope fully in Him with complete trust that He is good, has a plan for our lives, and will clothe us with salvation and righteousness (Isaiah 61:10). Romans 8 outlines for us several reasons why we can be people of hope. When we look at the benefits of the hope we have in Christ and the identities we receive because of Him, we have no reason for fear or hopelessness. Fear of God, the love of God, and hope in God, all of which we receive through a relationship with Him, are the vaccine to the fear virus. The more we study our reasons for hope, the stronger and healthier we will become.

I HAVE BEEN PARDONED

If you believe in Jesus, you should have confidence and hope because you have been pardoned by Christ. The Bible says this in Romans 8:1 (TLB), "There is now no condemnation awaiting those who belong to Christ Jesus." Notice that it did not say there are now no mistakes, there are now no failures, or there is now no sin. It says that there is no condemnation.

All of us mess up. Even the legendary leaders of faith took a tumble now and then. Abraham lied about his wife. David committed adultery with Bathsheba. Simon Peter denied knowing Christ three times in one night. Moses struck the rock in anger. None of these people experienced or suffered condemnation. But they did experience the consequences of sin. This is the key distinction in the Christian life. We are destined to come face to face with the consequences of our sin, but not condemnation for our sin.

You may have heard something similar to this as a child. Perhaps you have said this to your own children: "I am not going to punish you, but you will have to suffer the consequences of your actions." The whole world still groans under the consequences of what Adam and Eve did in the

Garden of Eden. Even though God, through Christ, has provided a way for us to be forgiven of sin, we still have to face the inevitable consequences of the sins of those who came before us.

In his letter to the Galatian Christians, Paul warns us that sin brings forth a harvest of destruction: "Do not be deceived: God cannot be mocked. A man reaps what he sows. Whoever sows to please their flesh, from the flesh will reap destruction; whoever sows to please the Spirit, from the Spirit will reap eternal life" (Galatians 6:7-8). When we make sinful choices, we are sowing seeds that will yield a crop of miserable consequences. God forgives, but He does not remove the inevitable fallout from our poor choices. He may choose to do that sometimes, but He will generally use the consequences of sin to teach us the joy of a spiritually disciplined life.

While we may have to deal with sin's consequences for a time, the great news is that there is no eternal condemnation for those who are in Christ. The word *condemnation* means punishment. We are never going to be punished for our sins if we are in Christ. Did you catch that? I will repeat that one more time. We are never going to be punished for our sins if we are in Christ. Is that good news or what? Talk about a benefit. That is unbelievable. Christ takes the penalty for our sin when we personally receive what He did for us on the cross. We are forever free from God's wrath, the righteous judgment of God for sin.

The Bible says in Hebrews 7:19, "But now we have a far better hope, for Christ makes us acceptable to God, and now we may draw near to him" (TLB). As a Christ follower, do you realize that God has accepted you because you have been pardoned? Because of this pardon, we may draw near to Him and we have access to the throne of God through the blood of His Son. We have been given the benefit of Christ's righteousness through faith. When He looks at us, God accepts us as clean, pure vessels.

One of the major causes of hopelessness is shame and guilt. Our enemy, Satan, likes to stuff our pockets with shame and guilt, even though he knows that we no longer stand condemned before God. He wants us to forget that we have been freed from punishment. He wants us to live in constant fear of the wrath of God, so we will lose our effectiveness as disciples. When we are still living in bondage to sin, we are not able to be effective witnesses for Christ and to experience the freedom we have in the Spirit.

Satan often whispers to us, "You are going to be punished for that. God will get you back for that one. He is going to hammer you. You had better look over your shoulder because one night you will be walking down the street and God will come up behind you and whack you." Satan is a liar. He is the father of lies and the greatest liar in the history of the world. He has been lying for thousands of years, and his strategy is to keep Christ-followers hemmed in and limited.

Satan works hard at keeping many of us who are in Christ in a state of hopelessness and fear. He whispers lies to us day in and day out. "You can't do that because of your past. God can't use you anymore because of what you did last week, last month or last year." We must call him a liar and remember we have been pardoned. We will suffer consequences, but we are not condemned. Christ took the punishment once and for all. It is over, signed, sealed, and delivered. Now we can go on and live our lives. We have an everlasting pardon from the Divine Judge of the universe.

WE HAVE THE POWER TO CHANGE

The second benefit of being a believer is that we have the power to change. Simply by being plugged into Jesus Christ, we have the power to make life-altering changes, become better people, and break free from the sin that entangles us. You may think that all people have the power to change within themselves, whether they are Christians or not. Everyone can make changes to some degree. But these are superficial and temporal changes that have nothing to do with the real inside-out kind of transformation that Christ offers. Only He can change the heart. Only He has power over sin and death. Only He can make us perfect by remaking us into His image.

A few years ago, I took a stress test. I stepped up on the treadmill and they started the test. The treadmill moved slowly at first, then faster and faster. The incline began to increase higher and higher. I was worn out after about twenty-five minutes, sweating profusely and gasping for air. My legs began to feel very heavy, as if I no longer had the strength to lift my feet off the treadmill's belt.

The doctor said, "Mr. Young, any time you want to stop just give me the nod, and I will push the stop button." I did not hesitate to respond, "I'm nodding. I'm nodding." He stopped the treadmill and I got off. I felt so much relief. I felt such freedom to finally be off that incessantly turning belt.

In a real sense, we are all on a treadmill called sin and death. Here is the cycle, how the belt turns on this spiritual treadmill. We are tempted, we fall, and we feel guilty. The incline gets ratcheted up in an unhealthy relationship, the belt begins to turn faster in a damaging habit, and the treadmill just keeps going. In desperation, we begin to realize that something is wrong inside and we don't really have the power to change that we thought we had. We say, "I can't change. I am powerless to change. I don't have anyone who can help me get off of this treadmill." But if you are in Christ, you do.

Paul tells us about this in Romans 8:2, "For the power of the life-giving Spirit—and this power is mine through Christ Jesus—has freed me from the vicious circle of sin and death" (TLB). What has control over you? What are you dealing with? If you know Christ personally, turn to Him and nod. Tell Him that you are tired, your legs are getting heavy, and you want to get off the treadmill. If you are in Christ, you can ask Him to give you the strength to take care of whatever difficulty you may be experiencing. And He will do it. Jesus Christ has freed us from the vicious cycle of sin. That is the second benefit of being a believer.

WE HAVE A PURPOSE FOR SUFFERING

The third benefit of the Christian life is that we have a purpose for suffering. We have been pardoned. We have the power to change. We have a purpose for suffering. The Bible says we will suffer. God does not promise an exemption from pain and suffering in the Christian life. James 1:2 is quite clear on this: "Whenever you face trials of many kinds . . ." The text does not say "if" but "when." Suffering is inevitable.

Life is full of problems. I know this is not a particularly profound statement. You know this as well as I do. You are most likely in the middle of a problem, coming out of a problem, or preparing for the next problem. That is life. It is easier to deal with the problems we face if we know that there is a greater purpose for them. The thing that really gets us down is when a problem occurs in our lives and we don't understand its meaning.

The Bible says that if we are in Christ, we understand and know the purpose behind suffering. Romans 8:28 is a popular verse for Christians: "And we know that God causes all things to work for good . . ." (NASB). Note the phrase *all things*. God is working in the midst of everything that happens, both good and bad. Does that mean divorce? Yes. Does that mean sickness? Yes. Does that mean death? Yes. Does that mean a financial setback? Yes. Does that mean the loss of a job? Yes. Does that mean a relational breakup? Yes. Does that mean relocation? Yes. He uses all things, good and bad, for a greater purpose. He does not intentionally cause bad things to happen to us, but He is able to use the problems of this fallen world for His glory and our growth.

A lot of people blame God for things that He shouldn't be blamed for. We live in a fallen world because God created us with the freedom to choose right or wrong. From the very beginning mankind has had a choice to follow the Lord or not. From the beginning, we have chosen to do wrong. Many of the negative experiences that we face in life are due to the fact that we, or others, have made incorrect choices. But we love to point the finger of blame at God when things go wrong. God is not responsible for the bad things that happen to us. Our own sin, the sin of others around us, and the sin of all those who came before us join together to produce a continuous shock wave of negative consequences in the world. God is not causing evil; He wants, through the power of the Holy Spirit, to restrain the evil that is so prevalent in the world.

God could erase sin at the snap of His fingers. In the blink of an eye, sin could be gone. Here is how He could do it: He could take away our freedom to choose. If we were unable to choose to go against God's will, there would be no sin. But we would be like a bunch of robots. God did not do that because He loves us and desires that we be able to love Him back—of our own free will.

What God does do is to cause all things, both good and bad, to work together for His ultimate glory and for our ultimate good. Look at the second part of that phrase in verse Romans 8:28, "to work together for good." "Work together" is an interesting concept in the original language. Its literal meaning in the Greek has to do with weaving. Have you ever done needlepoint? I am an arts and crafts kind of guy, and I have tried my hand at it. I've learned that if you look at the underside of needlepoint, it is ugly. The thread on the underside of the artwork has all kinds of knots in it. There is string dangling everywhere. If you were to just look at the underside of a piece of needlepoint, you would have very little appreciation for the beauty of the artwork. In fact, from your limited perspective, you would think it looks terrible. But if you turn it over, you see a completely different picture. All of those tangles and knots of thread on the underside work to create a tapestry of beauty that can only be seen from the top side of the fabric. From that vantage point, there is form to it, the colors come together, and it works visually in ways you would not have thought possible.

In life I often look at my own problems and those of others close to me from just my limited perspective. I look underneath the problems on the underside of the fabric and nothing makes sense. I tell God that I just don't understand what He is trying to do with all of this disarray. How is God going to make something beautiful out of all the knots and dangling thread? But God has a plan, and He asks that I trust Him to make something good out of the ugliness that I see. As I begin to see with the eyes of faith, then I begin to understand. I have faith that my life is beautiful in God's eyes, even though it might not always look that way to me now. It is a matter of perspective.

Think of something as evil and horrible as the crucifixion of Jesus Christ. The sinless Son of God was tortured. He hung there on the cross for our sins. God took something evil and made it into something incredible—the salvation of the world. You and I have been pardoned through the death of Christ. Good can come from even the greatest evil.

Let's look at the remainder of the passage from Romans 8:28: "God causes all things to work together for good to those who love God, to those who are called (*if you have a relationship with Christ*) according to *His* purpose" (NASB, parenthetical comment added). Even the trials, the evil things, and the bad circumstances of life fulfill a greater purpose for "those who are called according to His purpose." While we suffer for a little while from sin and a fallen world, we long for the plans and purposes of God to be fulfilled. Our suffering loosens the grip the world has on us because it gives us a longing for heaven. If you have been called by God and saved by God, your life will ultimately be fulfilled by God in eternity. All that you have experienced—good, bad, and ugly—will come together in a beautiful tapestry. Finally, you will be able to see what God sees as He looks down on the fine needlework in the fabric.

WE HAVE FREEDOM FROM OUR FEARS

The fourth reason why we should be the most hopeful people is the premise of this entire book. Simply put, we have freedom from our fears. Psychologists have identified over 645 different fears or phobias, and they are still counting. I listed several of those phobias in the introduction of this book, and we have already dealt in some detail with the three greatest fears that we face.

Not surprisingly, the number one fear is the fear of death. People are afraid to die and face the final chapter in their lives. We all have the desire to live because God gives us this desire. But eventually we are all going to die. If you are in Christ, there will be eternity in heaven for you. As Christians, there is nothing to fear about death. You can have hope: the salvation of your soul.

The second greatest fear we deal with is loneliness. I come in contact with so many lonely people. They have no real connectedness or community at work or in their neighborhood. They just don't know anyone in a real and authentic way. We all long for relationships because God has created us as relational beings. We cannot survive life on our own, as islands unto ourselves. We long for a personal relationship with Jesus Christ and for relationships with other human beings.

If you are in Christ, your relational base must be the church. The church has many points of entry, many avenues where you can meet some life-changing friends. In the church, you will find people who will surround you, love you, teach you, accept you, and forgive you. That is real community. When you share a common hope with others, you feel connected.

The third greatest fear is the fear of failure. We are fearful that if we step out, if we take a risk, if we try to challenge the unknown, or conquer this obstacle or fulfill that dream, we might fail. I have met so many people over the course of my ministry who are terrified of taking a risk and trying something new. They rationalize to God, "I can't try that because I may fall flat on my face." That is why the Bible has such a real and vibrant message for our lives today. The Bible gives me example after example of men and women who have fallen flat on their faces. These are real, flesh-and-blood people who have messed up—some of them big time. They have taken a risk, stumbled, and fallen, and yet God was able to pick up the pieces and use them in mighty ways.

I can identify with these ordinary men and women of the Bible. I fail all the time, and yet God still uses me. Jesus knows before it happens that we are going to fumble, fail, stumble, and fall. He knows, but He also tells us to get back up. He says, "I will forgive you. I will change you. I will work on you. And I will still use you." We should not fear failure because God makes His power known through imperfect vessels who are yielded to Him in faith and obedience. We can have hope that in our weakness, He is strong.

If you are outside of Christ, life can be scary. If you have not given your life to Christ, there is no one there to pick up the pieces. On the other hand, the Bible says this of those who are in Christ: "if God is for us, who can be against us?" (Romans 8:31). In this we hope and "since we have such a hope, we are very bold" (2 Corinthians 3:12). The Bible says "fear not" 365 times. That's one "fear not" for every day of the year. It is like God wanted that point to be obvious. So, fear not. If we are in Christ, we have freedom from our fears.

WE HAVE ETERNAL SECURITY

The fifth benefit of being a believer has to do with our eternal destiny. I have security forever through the person of Jesus Christ, who embodies the final hope of the believer. All of us have a longing for eternity. We saw earlier in Ecclesiastes that the desire for eternity has been placed in our hearts. Have you ever wondered why most little children's books end with, "and they lived happily ever after?" We have this desire for a happy ending. When we go see a movie and it has a bad ending, we don't like the movie because the ending leaves a bad taste in our mouths. God has set eternity in our hearts and an unhappy ending does not compute with what we know in our hearts is supposed to happen.

Have you ever been reading a novel, and it gets so exciting that you have to flip to the last chapter to see the ending in order to relieve the tension? I did that recently. I just couldn't take the suspense. If we are in Christ, we have read the last chapter. God has already revealed the final page. We win. We spend eternity with Jesus.

The moment you accept Jesus Christ as your Savior, He will not let go. You might wiggle and squirm from time to time and even spend part of your Christian life in rebellion, trying to pull away, but He will not let go. This is a forever deal: "Neither death nor life, neither angels nor demons, neither the present nor the future, nor any powers, neither height nor depth, nor anything else in all creation, will be able to separate us from the love of God that is in Christ Jesus our Lord" (Romans 8:38-39).

SO WHAT?

Let me ask you a two-word question: "So what?" You have seen the reasons for hope. You know that hope is a person, Jesus Christ, and you have no reason to fear if you are in Christ. You have read about the benefits of the Christian life as a result of the hope that we have through Christ. But, so what? Let me give you something that will help you apply these principles in your daily life.

Always be prepared to share your hope with others. The Book of 1 Peter says it like this: "But in your hearts revere Christ as Lord. Always be prepared to give an answer to everyone who asks you to give the reason for the hope that you have. But do this with gentleness and respect" (1 Peter 3:15). If your life reflects the benefits of being a believer, people will ask you, "Why are you that way? Why do you have joy? Why do you have confidence, even when it is tough for you, even when you have just lost a loved one or broken off a relationship? Why do you have this peace in the midst of your tears? How do you do it?" The world will give you a window to share what you believe.

Have you ever shared about Jesus Christ with others? Sadly, the world today is more prepared to receive this message than many of us are willing to give it. Are you reflecting confidence and hope in every area of your life? People are watching. They are checking you out.

If we meditate on the Word of God, feed on the benefits of being a believer, and know who we are in Christ, the world can look at us and see our joy, confidence, and fearlessness. They will see our joy and hope because it will be reflected in how we treat others. What are you feeding on? The world's garbage or the Bread of Life? If you are prepared to share the hope you have with others and are meditating daily on the benefits of believing in God's Word, you will know the mystery that has been revealed in Christ—a hope that never fails.

CHAPTER 10

THE FINAL WORD

PERFECT LOVE

A while back, I was speaking on stage at Fellowship Church using a Bible my parents had given me when I was young. I had forgotten that I had saved a love letter from Lisa inside the Bible that she wrote me when I was eighteen years old.

She wrote, "Dear Edwin B. (my middle name is Barry) I think about you all of the time, and that's the truth. All I can do is think about the time when I'll be with you again. I hope that will be soon, because it seems like a month until I last saw you . . ." (It's getting hot, I can't read you the rest.) ". . . Love, always and forever, Lisa."

It's fitting that this love letter was tucked in my Bible because that is what the Bible is—a huge love letter to you and me. In fact, God is love. "Wait a minute, Ed. I thought you said earlier in the book that the chief quality of God is His holiness." Everything flows from His holiness. His love is a holy love, and love is the final word on fear.

We have already seen from our study on the fear of God that "perfect love drives out fear" (1 John 4:18). It is fitting to end this book on fear with an in-depth look at biblical love. When we truly understand God's love for us, we aren't susceptible to the fear virus that runs rampant in our society. We can look in the face of fear, knowing that we are overcomers and that God—the God of love—is on our side.

There is a lot of confusion about love these days. Some people confuse love with an emotion. They say that love is a feeling. Love is not a feeling or an emotion. Love causes feelings and it causes emotions, but love is neither a feeling nor an emotion. God commands us to love Him and others, but He does not command feelings. Feelings cannot be commanded or demanded. As an earthly father, I can't say to my children, "Kids, I command you to be happy." They would probably reply, "We're trying. We're trying to be happy, Dad." But, if they do not feel happy, all the trying in the world is not going to make them have feelings of happiness. The same is true for love. Love is much more than a feeling or an emotion.

Other people confuse love with lust. Love is not lust. Lust cannot wait to get, while love cannot wait to give. For many people these days, love is pseudo-love or thinly veiled selfishness. We like to make this magnanimous statement: "I love you." But if you read the fine print, we're actually saying, "I'll love you if you meet my needs, do what I want, and show me affection. But the moment you stop doing that, I am jumping to Tinder and finding someone new."

People talk about falling in love like they talk about falling into a swimming pool. Popular culture feeds this idea just about everywhere we turn. But love, according to the Author of love, is a decision. The Bible explodes all of this confusion and nails it down precisely in 1 John 3:18: "Little children, let us stop saying we love people; let us really love them, and show it by our actions" (TLB). Love is a choice and it always reveals itself in action.

Here is what God wants to do in our lives. God loves us so much that He wants to take us from the natural realm of loving into the supernatural realm of loving. God wants to do that, and He will do it, if we can answer two important questions about love and incorporate these answers into our lives.

HOW DOES GOD EXPRESS
HIS LOVE FOR ME?

The first question is: How does God express His love for me? If you are married, think back to the time you were dating. For some it might be a longer jaunt down memory lane than for others. Do you remember those "statements at the door"? You walk her to the door, and you take the risk and say, "I really had a nice time tonight." You are hoping and praying that she returns the sentiment by saying, "I had a nice time, too." And if you get past that hurdle, you think, "Oh boy, I'm cruising now."

A couple of weeks later, you face the next hurdle. You begin to get a little more vulnerable and say something like, "I really enjoy being with you." You wait anxiously, and hopefully she says it back. Then when she does, you get in the car and shout, "Yes!"

As you spend more time together, you are starting to realize that you love her and you know it is just a matter of time before you will have to say that three-word sentence, that high-risk pronouncement.

The time finally comes. You see her, your palms are sweaty, and your heart is racing. You look into her eyes and begin to work up to it: "You are incredible." You know you have to say it. But, if you say it and she rejects it, you will be devastated. Still, you realize that you must be real and honest. You must be true to your feelings. You must take the risk. You come to that point when you look into her eyes and say, "I love you." You've unloaded the tremendous weight from your chest, the cards are on the table, you have shown your hand, and you have taken the mystery out of the relationship. Then, to your great relief and delight, she responds to your bold pronouncement by saying, "I love you, too."

God makes this high-risk pronouncement right out of the gate. He doesn't have to work up to it or wait for the right cues from us before He takes the risk. God comes right out and says it. Even though He knows we might reject it, even though He knows we might spurn it, even though He knows we might turn our back on it, God says it over and over again: "I love you. I love you. I love you." When you make a statement like that, you have to back it up because love costs something. God didn't just stop with saying, "I love you." He actually put it in bold print. He went on record in the Book, the Bible.

He writes it down. The first way God expresses His love to us is through documentation. He has written it down. God has written it down over and over again, so people will never waver on the point. We don't have to wonder or speculate. He writes things like this to us in Isaiah 43:1, "Do not fear, for I have redeemed you; I have called you by name; you are Mine!" (NASB). In Romans 5:8, He declares, "God demonstrates His love toward us, in that while we were yet sinners, Christ died for us" (NASB). In Jeremiah 31:3 He says, "I have loved you with an everlasting love; I have drawn you with loving-kindness." God assures us repeatedly that His love will never run out.

I have talked over the years to many people who tell me they have committed a sin that has broken the back of God's love. People really believe they can bankrupt the love of God. And I love to point them to this passage: "I have loved you with an everlasting love." The Bible says that God *is* love, so He cannot walk away from love any more than He can walk away from Himself. His very nature reaches out to us and extends love and forgiveness no matter how bad we've blown it, no matter what we think we've done that would cause Him to stop loving us.

We are talking about love in a supernatural realm. We can't possibly completely comprehend the depths of God's love because our finite minds are incapable of calculating God's infinite character qualities. While God has a kind of love that we cannot comprehend, we can receive it and count on it as much as we count on God Himself.

He illustrates it. God also expresses His love for us through illustration. He uses a great variety of word pictures to communicate, express, and illustrate His love for us.

God uses nature and animals throughout the Bible to illustrate different truths and aspects of His character. In Matthew 23:37, for example, Jesus says, "How often I have longed to gather your children together, as a hen gathers her chicks under her wings." God talks about His love in Proverbs by comparing it to the love a lioness or a bear has for her cubs. In Psalm 103:11, "For as high as the heavens are above the earth, so great is His loving-kindness for those who fear him" (NASB).

God also illustrates His love through parental pictures. If you are a mother, Isaiah 49:15 might connect with you: "Can a mother forget the baby at her breast and have no compassion on the child she has borne? Though she may forget, I will not forget you!" If you are a father, Psalm 103:13 may be for you: "As a father has compassion on his children, so the Lord has compassion on those who fear Him."

If you have a best friend who means a lot to you, you might connect with a picture of the love one friend has for another. Christ says in John 15:13, "Greater love has no one than this: to lay down one's life for one's friends."

Paul also uses sports illustrations like in 2 Timothy 4:7-8 which says, "I have fought a good fight. I have finished the work I was to do. I have kept the faith. There is a crown which comes from being right with God. The Lord, the One Who will judge, will give it to me on that great day when He comes again. I will not be the only one to receive a crown. All those who love to think of His coming and are looking for Him will receive one also" (NLT). James 1:12 says, "Blessed is the one who perseveres under trial because, having stood the test, that person will receive the crown of life that the Lord has promised to those who love him." God uses a variety of illustrations and descriptions to bring home to each of us a word picture of His great love for us.

He demonstrates it. It is great that God has told me this, but how does He show it? How does God really reveal His love for us? How does He express it? Remember, God expresses it through documentation and illustration. Most significantly, though, God also expresses His love for us in practice. God's love is not just a bunch of rhetoric or a nice little story to make us feel warm and fuzzy. God has taken His love to the mat. He has shown us His love in many tangible ways. He has truly demonstrated His love to humanity.

Take a quick glance through history. God demonstrated His love to Adam and Eve. After they sinned, He gave them a second chance. Look at Noah and his family. They were about to get into some serious flood problems, but God delivered them and saved them because of His love. Abraham was going to sacrifice his son Isaac, and God demonstrated His love to Abraham by providing a ram in place of his son. When David committed adultery with Bathsheba, God demonstrated His love to David by forgiving him.

You could go on and on through the pages of Scripture until you come to God's ultimate demonstration of His love in the person and work of Jesus. God expressed His love in the most profound way possible by sending Jesus Christ. He left His home in heaven, put on flesh, humbled Himself to the place of suffering, and got knocked around on the playing field of life. God offered Jesus Christ, His precious only Son, as a sin sacrifice for undeserving people like us. The cross stands as the ultimate symbol of God's love.

One of the most quoted passages in all the Bible says it best: "For God so loved the world, that He gave His only begotten Son, that whoever believes in Him shall not perish, but have eternal life" (John 3:16, NASB). But it doesn't end there because God gets specific. God tells us throughout the pages of Scripture, "I have loved you since you were born. I have reached out to you. I have offered guidance. I have offered you salvation. I have offered you a home in heaven. You are mine, and my love is right there for you. You either receive it or you don't."

We do one of two things with God's love. We either receive God's love or we reject God's love. It is as simple as that. For those of us who receive God's love, we open up our hearts and discover a love so wide, high, and deep that it is only natural for us to want to return God's love by giving Him our time, abilities, talents, and treasures. It is a natural thing to love God and to want to express our feelings of love and gratitude toward Him.

But many people have rejected God's love. They have turned their backs to it, explained it away, or put it off. The only way we can truly love others and truly love ourselves is by accepting God's love, letting it wash over us and make us whole. When we reject God's love, we are also rejecting hope, joy, and abundance. Only He can satisfy us and quell our fears.

God doesn't force His love on us. But He continually offers opportunities to accept His perfect love into our lives. His love is the antidote to fear. It's water in the desert, food to starving souls. God endlessly expresses His love to us. He has put it in writing. He has illustrated it and demonstrated it. I will ask again the question that I have been asking throughout this book: Have you received it?

HOW DO I EXPRESS GOD'S LOVE TO OTHERS?

Let's jump to the next important question about God's love. If I am in contact with God's love, how do I express this love to others? I have this love that is so phenomenal. I have discovered it. I have accepted it. I am returning it to God. How do I express it to others?

Service. God says that we express God's love to others by serving them. Love and service are inseparably linked. The Bible says that all of us have unique abilities and talents. God gives us spiritual and natural gifts to be used for His glory and in service to others. If you are connected with a local church, you see these gifts and talents played out on a weekly basis. You see people with the gift of teaching every time you hear a life-changing message or participate in a Bible study or class. You see others using their artistic abilities, musical talent, gift of encouragement, or gift of organization. God has blessed us with gifts. He wants us to bless others by using our gifts, by serving others, and by getting involved in people's lives.

Christians talk a lot about serving God. "Service" is one of the spiritual buzzwords in the church. Many people are actually doing it in various ministries within the church. You may be involved in your church in the children's ministry, sound and lighting, or small group ministry. You are putting action behind your words. You are serving others. On a more personal level, though, are you serving the people closest to you on a daily basis? Are you serving your spouse? Are you serving your children? Are you serving the people you work with and work for? Do you have an attitude of service twenty-four hours a day and seven days a week?

Jesus articulated one of the great ironies of spiritual greatness in Mark 9:35: "If anyone wants to be first, he must be the very last, and a servant of all." If you want to be great, you must become a servant.

I am going to give you an assignment to bring this section home on a practical level. For the next seven days, do one act of service secretly each day for one person (or more if you're an overachiever). You may choose your spouse as the recipient of your "secret service." Or maybe your children. Maybe you are thinking of a friend or mentor or coworker. Bless them in some way over the next week. Find ways to serve them. Maybe you can send someone twenty dollars just because. Maybe you can bake a cake for your kids or watch your spouse's favorite movie with them even though you don't like it. Show the love of Christ to the people in your life—remind them that they are loved by God and by you.

Commitment. Love should also express itself through commitment. We must be committed. Love and commitment, like love and service, go hand in hand. How many people these days say they have decided just to live together so they can test the waters? Later, if their trial run works out, they will get married. This is not love. This is affection. Love is commitment. It is not afraid of the risk. Love says to the other person, "I am going to hang in there even though I don't feel like it all the time. I am committed to you."

The same is true in your commitment to the other people in your family, your work, your friendships, and your church. When was the last time you verbalized your commitment to a friend or coworker, someone special to you, someone you are with daily? When was the last time you committed to a local body of Christ? Many people show up every week to church and get fed from the Word of God but aren't truly connected. Maybe it is time for you to make a commitment—I mean a real commitment. The Bible commands us to be a part of the local body of Christ: "Let us not give up meeting together, as some are in the habit of doing, but encouraging one another—and all the more as you see the Day approaching" (Hebrews 10:25). In our world today, meeting together can be done easier than in anytime in human history. So, no excuses! Email or call your church, go online, and fill out a form to get connected. I know the pastors and staff there would be more than happy to connect with you and connect you with others. Don't wait; get connected today!

There are several good reasons to make a commitment to

the church, not the least of which is a biblical reason: Christ is committed to His church, and He wants the same from us. There is also a cultural reason: the church has the antidote for the deep moral problems and fears that plague our society. Community is there to walk with you through every season, struggle, battle, and fear. You'll never experience anything better than being committed with all of your strength, passion, and resources to the body of Christ.

Sacrifice. Another way we express love is through sacrifice. Sacrifice means to give the best we have for a better purpose. Are you living out sacrificial love? Are you giving the best you have for a greater purpose? Are you giving your best, even though someone will not pat you on the back, even though it is really going to cost you something?

It hurts to give sacrificially. That is the point of the exercise of sacrificial giving. When we give sacrificially, it communicates to God and others our priorities in life. We are giving up certain things that are less important in order to contribute to and build up things that are more important. Paul describes the gifts he received from the Philippian church to support his ministry as an "acceptable sacrifice" in Philippians 4:18: "I have received from Epaphroditus the gifts you sent. They are a fragrant offering, an acceptable sacrifice, pleasing to God."

Maybe giving sacrificially means putting some purchases on hold. It might mean deciding that you don't need to own certain things. It might mean choosing to spend less on Christmas gifts so you can give sacrificially to the eternal work of the church or ministries that are doing God's work. That kind of sacrificial giving is making a lasting impression on the lives of our children. They will reflect what they see modeled. Sacrificial love is one of the cornerstones of the Christian life—it is how we most look like Jesus.

Sharing. Another way we express love is by sharing the faith and hope we have with others. One of the most loving things you can do is to share the Lord Jesus Christ with others. Share with them what the Lord has done in your life. Love gives us no other option. Paul says that the love of Christ "compels us" to share the gospel of Christ with others and to help bring reconciliation between them and God (2 Corinthians 5:14). We must be committed to what Christ was committed to, and Christ was committed to people. He loved people and He said that we are to be committed to and love people. Are you loving people? Are you sharing the Bread of Life with people? Are you sharing the light of God's truth in a dark and fearful world?

Jesus said in the Sermon on the Mount that we cannot hide the light that is in us any more than a city set on a hill can be hidden. "You are the light of the world. A town built on a hill cannot be hidden. Neither do people light a lamp and put it under a bowl. Instead they put it on its stand, and it gives light to everyone in the house. In the same way, let your light shine before others, that they may see your good deeds and glorify your Father in heaven" (Matthew 5:14-16). The light of God's truth is meant to shine in the darkness, not to be hidden within the four walls of the church or our home. The Bread of Life is meant to be shared with others so they can come to the light and experience the love of God.

1 Corinthians 13:13 says, "These three things remain: faith, hope, and love. But the greatest of these is love." I have to admit that this text puzzled me for a long time. Why does the Bible say that the greatest of the three is love? We have taken a look throughout this book at the various ways that faith, hope, and love are antidotes to our earthly fears. But why is love the greatest?

Here is why I believe love is the greatest of the three. One day when we get to heaven, we won't need any more faith because we will see the Lord face to face. As for hope, who needs hope once everything we have hoped for is finally realized? On that day, every need will be met, every fear vanquished, and every dream realized to the tenth power and beyond. The only thing that will remain is love. This love will never leave you because God Himself is the ultimate embodiment of pure and true love. Love is the final word on fear because God's perfect love casts out all fear. His love sustains us now and forever. And perfect love is always found in Jesus.

ABOUT THE AUTHOR

Ed Young is the founding and senior pastor of Fellowship Church, with locations in Texas, Florida, Oklahoma, and Online at FellowshipLive.com. As a noted author, Ed has written 15 books, including his most recent book, Amazon bestseller *Fifty Shades Of They,* and New York Times bestseller *Sexperiment.* Other books by Ed Young include *Outrageous, Contagious Joy, Beauty Full,* and *Kid CEO.*

Ed is a frequent conference speaker, and he provides resources and leadership coaching for church leaders through CreativePastors.com and the Creative Church Conferences (C3). You can find his messages, devotionals, and designs at EdYoung.com.

Ed has been married to his wife, Lisa, for more than thirty years. They have four children and live in the Dallas/Fort Worth area.